WE DARE TO SAY OUR FATHER

WE DARE TO SAY
OUR FATHER

LOUIS EVELY

HERDER
FREIBURG

PALM PUBLISHERS
MONTREAL

Original edition

"Notre Père — Aux sources de notre fraternité",

Editions Fleurus, Paris. Translated by James Langdale

1st Edition 1965

2nd Impression 1965

3rd Impression 1965

4th Impression 1965

5th Impression 1965

6th Impression 1965

7th Impression 1966

8th Impression 1966

————

2nd Edition 1967

Nihil Obstat: Joannes M. T. Barton, S. T. D., L. S. S.,

Censor deputatus

Imprimatur: † Georgius L. Craven, Epus. Sebastopolis, Vic. Gen.

Westmonasterii, die 24ª Aug., 1964

First published in West Germany © 1965 Herder KG

Printed in West Germany by Herder

PALM PUBLISHERS, 1949—55th Ave., Dorval-Montreal

Contents

Except the Father draw him

"No MAN can come to me, except the Father, who hath sent me, draw him."[1] What is it that has drawn us to this retreat? Why are we here? We must begin with an act of faith. We must believe that we have been impelled by a supernatural influence, that God wanted us to be here, even if we are under the impression that we couldn't do otherwise, even if we are furious at the idea of being here — "What on earth brought me to this place!" — even if we are sorely tempted to run away.

Who on earth brought us to this place? Someone. No one comes of his own volition. Not even Christ: "I did not come of my own will." It is always the Father who draws, who sends. But once he has drawn us to him, he will not drop us. Once, in a mood of intense sadness, Jesus said to his disciples, "You will leave me alone." But he corrected himself at once, "I am not alone but I and the Father that sent me."[2] We too should also say that to ourselves: "I will not be alone; the Father will be with me."

"I hear within myself something like a sound of

[1] John 6:44. [2] John 8:16.

1

running water which says: Come to the Father", wrote St. Ignatius of Antioch as he prepared for martyrdom. This is the only valid reason for staying; we would find all others wanting. Rightly so, we would find all others inadequate. All others would not prevent us from running away. One thing only is beyond argument; I have not come of my own volition. I have not come to do my own will. The Father has overcome me. Be it done to me...

"In those days again, when there was a great multitude and they had nothing to eat; calling his disciples together, he saith to them: I have compassion on the multitude, for behold they have now been with me three days and have nothing to eat. And if I shall send them away fasting to their home, they will faint in the way: for some of them came from afar off. And his disciples answered him: From whence can one fill them here with bread in the wilderness?"[3]

At a retreat too, there are some who come from afar. And how are we to find enough bread to feed them? "I have compassion . . . they have now been with me three days." We are going to spend six, seven days with him. He will certainly have compassion on us. We must have trust in him, even if we feel that we are really in a wilderness — of loneliness, weariness, fatigue. At that time they had seven loaves for four thousand men. "And he commanded the people to sit down on the ground . . . And they did eat and were filled."

Everything began with an act of faith. Did you notice the order that Jesus gave, the condition he stipulated before he made the miracle? "Sit down." He asked them for an act of trust, renunciation, surrender into his hands.

[3] Mark 8:1-4.

So long as they remained standing, there was a chance that they might manage to feed themselves. They might meet a friend, a pedlar carrying food, go to an inn or find some fruit. They were free to leave. But the very moment they sat down, they would have given up the idea of being self-sufficient, of being able to fend for themselves; they would be at his mercy.

I am sure that many hesitated when they heard this call. He asked them precisely for what cost them most, for the thing they did not want to do. They were excited, worried, tortured by hunger, and he asked them to sit down and trust him. For a long time they hesitated. The fullness of his demand drove deep into their hearts and wrestled within them with their fear and pride. Were they going to trust him? Were they going to believe that he was able to feed them?

Some, making a tremendous act of faith, sat down; and with a supreme effort they closed their eyes as if they had given, as if they had lost their lives. Then others, gasping, overcome, deeply moved, followed them. Great portions of the crowd shuddered and gave way. Then there was an extraordinary moment, a miraculous moment, when the four thousand sat down: when four thousand men together made an act of faith and love.

And when the bread was passed round amongst them and all had received their fill and there was still some left — no one was surprised. The real miracle had happened; it had already taken place. Jesus had secured from them the greatest miracle of all: the miracle of their faith, their love.

When we come to a retreat our luggage contains some books, some unanswered letters, chocolate, work, a railway timetable (just in case things become unbearable), some food, and in any case enough to make us self-sufficient. And the Lord asks us to believe that he will be sufficient for us, that he can feed us, satisfy us, entertain us for six days. That he loves us enough to gratify all our wishes and that he has enough life in him to make us live of him for six days.

We experience the same anguish as that crowd to which a similar miracle was proposed. Will we, like them, manage to sit down quietly, wait, give up living our own life to live of his?

The growth of spiritual life follows somewhat the same rule as that of lobsters. When lobsters grow, their shell inevitably becomes too tight, too small for them; they need another. Then they experience a terrifying moment. The shell bursts and they are left bruised and stripped of their covering which hurt but nevertheless protected them. To go into retreat means giving up our usual shelter to go and expose ourselves to the sting of brine, to the surf, to the stiff breeze of the high seas (instructions, prayers) so as to grow a new and larger shell.

When we go on a retreat, we give up action. This, naturally, is not enough. We must, of course, not come to the conclusion that as prayer is more efficacious than anything else, all that we need do is to pray — thy kingdom come! — and do nothing else. We are going to relearn how to pray in order to relearn how to live. But between these two extremes: prayer and action, there are the steps which we must take in order to bind together those two parts of our lives.

The purpose of a retreat is to adjust these steps and it enables us to go back into action with the peaceful and smiling gravity of an envoy. "It is the Father that sends me." But to do this we must first have found the Father again. We must have given ourselves to him, placed ourselves in his hands. "They have nothing to eat." Do we agree only to eat what he will give us? Shall we have the courage to place ourselves before him in such a void, in such poverty, trust, and faith?

God also asks us for silent reflection. We must be very careful here because it is the very reverse of introspection. A retreat is not an exercise in solipsism. We are already far too much alone! On the contrary, we must rediscover truth by returning into communion with God and others. To reflect silently means to accept to be ourselves again, to re-exist. And *ex-sistere* means getting out of ourselves.

We all have an infernal love of annihilation; we are perpetually tempted not to be, to destroy ourselves, to commit suicide, to cut ourselves off from a certain communion outside which we know there is no life. Pride consists in relying on our own strength, in wanting to cease relying on all those things and people who hurt us, to cut ourselves off from all those forces that make for communion, community, brotherhood — that would give us life, though beforehand we would have to accept death.

When we recollect in silence, we agree to rediscover our grievous and profound solidarity with everyone around us. In silence and humility we rediscover what God does within us. Silent recollection means going back to the fountainhead. Once more we know what we are, provided we go back whence we came. Often, the mouth of a river is no more than a muddy and shapeless sheet of water. If we want to know the taste of that water, the name of that river, we must go back and search for it whence it came.

We come from God; and we only exist in God. We

5

need humility — and not pride as some think — to believe this, to believe that we are destined to become God. To admire ourselves within Another. To accept to be entirely dependent on Another, to be happy only through Another.

Through silent recollection, we must rediscover in ourselves the model in whose image we have been created. This will take time. It will be slow. We will need much patience. Often the light of God comes like neon lighting: there is an interval between the time when we turn on the switch and the time when the light blazes upon us. If we become impatient, if we cannot bear to remain faithful in the dark for as long as it is necessary, if we turn furiously upon our heels and say "nothing doing", God cannot enlighten us. We must not turn the switch off or get excited. We must keep calm and recollected. Then, within a few hours or a few days, a shudder will sometimes pass through the tubes, we will see a few sparks. And then, suddenly, the light will be there.

Let us begin our retreat with an act of faith: God is going to give. God is going to give something to us. God is going to give us what we need. The Father is going to speak to us, he is going to say to us the word that he has meant for us from all eternity.

No doubt we will act like Samuel who began by doing exactly what should not be done. Hearing the call that urged him to listen and be silent, he rushed — to his work, his boss, his adviser, everywhere except where God wanted him — to find out what he should do. "Now Samuel did not yet know the Lord; neither had the word of the Lord been revealed to him. And the Lord called Samuel again the third time. And he arose up [for the third time] and went to Heli. And said: Here am I; for thou didst call me. Then Heli understood that the Lord

6

called the child, and he said to Samuel: Go, and sleep. And if he shall call thee any more, thou shalt say: Speak Lord, for thy servant heareth. So Samuel went and slept in his place."[4] Keep still, Samuel. Keep quiet. Just say, "Speak Lord, for thy servant heareth". It is a good prayer. And stop moving about. Surrender yourself. Give yourself up to this word which will only come to you if you give yourself up silently, entirely, to what it wants of you. However powerful the Lord might be, he could not get Samuel to hear him until Samuel agreed to be quiet, to be attentive, until he gave him time to reach him.

God's visits go so deep that often we are not aware of them until they have taken place. The disciples of Emmaus did not recognize him until he was about to leave them, or — to be more precise — until he had finished manifesting himself to them. For he is always with us.

Newman wrote: "We come, like Jacob, in the dark, and lie down with a stone for our pillow; but when we rise again and call to mind what has passed, we recollect we have seen a vision of angels, and the Lord manifested through them, and we are led to cry out, 'How dreadful is this place! This is none other than the house of God, and this is the gate of heaven'."[5]

Faith, recollection. Availability. We must place ourselves at God's disposal, abide his time. His thoughts are not our thoughts. His ways are not our ways. To follow his, we must cast ours away. We must unburden ourselves. Blessed are the clean of heart for they shall see God.

We come to God full of questions, full of problems.

[4] 1 Kings 3:7-9.
[5] Parochial & Plain Sermons. Vol 4. London, 1868, pp. 264, 265.

Let us be silent. Unless we stop putting questions, we will be unable to hear his answers. All our questions, all our anxieties, all our grievances spring from the same cause: God is not God for us. We have invented one made to our own image. Stubbornly, we persist in addressing ourselves to the idea which we have conceived of God. It is not surprising that it should deceive us.

"I confess to thee, O Father, Lord of heaven and earth, because thou hast hidden these things from the wise and prudent and hast revealed them to little ones."[6] To the poor. To those who have the soul of a poor man. To those who are unburdened.

Heaven will be to see how God is God. But heaven can begin on earth. God is the Word; he reveals himself to us continually. Above all he wishes to communicate with us. Man's hunger for God is as nothing compared with God's hunger for man. We would not be searching for him if he had not already found us.

Because he has begun it, he will finish his work in us. We must not be afraid. He hurts us. He tears us apart, we feel we are dying; this is good; he is taking effect. "Unless the seed dieth . . ." Something in our life must alter after a retreat. But we must not know beforehand what this is to be. Otherwise it is not God who is working within us.

God will work within those who have the soul of a poor man, who have forsaken their questions, their ideas, their "idea of holiness", who no longer know anything and who place their trust in him. God's ideas on all this are vastly different from ours. Let us cast ours aside, lest they screen what God wishes to suggest to us. We are all gasping un-

[6] Luke 10:21.

der a burden which we have usurped. "Be you humbled under the mighty hand of God."[7]

To pray is to place ourselves at God's disposal, so that he may do with us what he wanted to do from the beginning of time. To pray is to become once more a son, docile, attentive. God tempts us and we allow ourselves to be tempted. Do we want to be "brothers"? Let us become sons once more. It is only when we are subject to a common father that we are brothers. To become brothers we have only to become sons again.

The first word that should be said, perhaps the only one that should be said, is: "Behold the handmaid of the Lord; be it done to me according to thy word."[8] Absolute faith. "Be it done to me . . ." Complete surrender.

[7] 1 Peter 5:6.
[8] Luke 1:38.

We make bold to say

WHEN JESUS was asked, "Lord, teach us to pray", Jesus replied: "You will say: Our Father, who art in Heaven, hallowed be thy Name . . ."

And since then, every day, thousands and thousands of Christians, "urged by our Saviour's bidding and schooled by his divine ordinance", have made bold to say: "Our Father . . . ."

For a week we are going to learn how to pray the prayer of the Lord, allowing ourselves to be schooled to this sacrifice of praise. All the precepts of the Lord, "the biddings of the Saviour", teach it to us, the whole of the Mass leads us to it, the whole life and death of the Lord take us to it — "schooled by his divine ordinance" — school us to it, shape us to it.

No one knows how to say, Father. Do not think that you know how to say: "Our Father". Only Christ, only the Son knows how to say, Father. In the centre of the Mass, in the centre of the real "Imitation of Jesus Christ", after we have allowed ourselves to be moulded according to the most profound intentions of the heart of Christ, we pause and we say: "We make bold . . ." And then we attempt to say: "Our Father".

Our

Outside a brotherhood, outside a solidarity, it is not possible to say the Our Father. Give us *our* daily bread . . . forgive us *our* trespasses. God willed a community, even of bread, even of sins. Thus God has taught us that a filial prayer is necessarily a brotherly one and that to be sons we must be brothers. If a son leaves his brothers, he is no longer a son. If he withdraws from the community, if he cuts himself adrift, he also ceases to be a son of God. For he no longer looks like God.

In God, they are three who love each other. God is a community of persons; God is effusion. And men have been made in the image of God. We cannot be Father all on our own. We cannot be Son all on our own. We cannot be Spirit of exchange and love all on our own. They are several in God. If we ceased to be brothers, if we were separate beings, we would be in the image of a lonely God.

"Communicantes . . ." Recollection is the return of all our capacity for communion. By becoming once more ourselves in the most profound sense of the word, we become again profoundly affable, sociable. Humanity meets when saying the Our Father. It takes back its real shape by becoming like him who made it in his image. The greatest

service we can render a human being is to offer it a face in which it can recognize and accept itself. In the first Christian communities, humanity recognized itself.

Humanity was converted to Christianity when it saw people who loved one another. "See how they love one another." They recognized each other. They found each other again. They rediscovered their true countenance as men, children of God, as they watched the life of these small brotherhoods of people who loved one another. They became themselves again by loving too.

Usually we believe that to be ourselves we must above all assert ourselves, free ourselves, become self-sufficient, have no need of others. We fail to see that this effort is really an exercise in self-destruction. What is the use of being our own master if we are incapable of giving ourselves to others? The true conquest of self is to offer ourselves to others. We become truly ourselves, only when together with others we reach a certain depth of communion, sharing, and exchange with them.

If man had been created all alone, if he had not been able to say "our" — our Father — he would not have been made in the image of God. From the beginning, God made man and woman, more than one then, so that they might love one another. We know not God if we know not love. We know not God if we do not become God. We will only know God when we have allowed him to grow within us. We will only know God if we have received him, if we have made room for him, if we have left room for him.

If all that God had given us were gifts to be received, he would have given us nothing of himself. If God had only given us the gift of being loved, he would have given us nothing of his own life. Because God loves, God gives.

But "everyone that loveth, is born of God, and knoweth

12

God".[1] Whoever is loved without loving is a pitiable beggar, a man who is half-dead. Whereas he who loves without being loved, who loves more generously, more keenly with greater suffering than he is loved . . . that man is "like God". To him it is given to know the taste of God, God's way of loving, the love of God.

Before we commune with the Body of God, we are ordered to make our peace with one another: "If therefore thou offer thy gift at the altar, and there thou remember that thy brother hath anything against thee; leave there thy offering before the altar, and go first to be reconciled to thy brother; and then coming thou shalt offer thy gift."[2] Since you want to become a son, start first by becoming a brother again. Come back to be a son since you want to be a brother. We must never disassociate these two essential aspects of our Christian life. The tragedy of our generous but desperate age is that we want a brotherhood without a Father.

But it is even more tragic to watch the so-called Christians who want fatherhood without brotherhood, who want to be sons of the Father without being brothers of the other sons. It is no fault of the unbelievers if they err. They have not been told of these things. But the same cannot be said of us! "Urged by our Saviour's bidding, schooled . . . we make bold to say, Our Father."

Nothing is more dismal, more frigid than some religious ceremonies, than that absence of communication which we have come to look upon as the normal thing. In church, our chairs are real insulators. One says one's own prayers. There is more communion in a railway carriage than at some of our Sunday Masses. There, at least, people talk

[1] 1 John 4:7.   [2] Matt. 5:23-24.

a little, offer each other fruit, exchange papers. At Mass, too often, each one of us keeps to *his* missal, carefully shrouding his impressions with polite silence. This goes on until the time for "communion" and then, each man for himself, we edge along, we shove, we even manage sometimes to steal four places ahead, and then we come back to resume our solitary meditation, covering our eyes with our fists, the better to isolate ourselves — Let no one touch me! Leave me alone! *I* am communicating; (You are excommunicating yourself!) I am saying *my* prayer, *Our* Father!

A Christian is known by the love he bears his brothers. "By this shall all men know..." Why was Jesus so emphatic? Because the love of God is more difficult to discern than the love of brothers. Because, when we love God, we are never able to disentangle what is free from what is not, what is love and what is not. It is not possible for our love of God not to be to our own advantage. To make sure, nevertheless, that it is love, we must not only love him but love like him. And when we say that we love God, we are never sure that it is true. We can, according to our whim, bring nearer into or farther out of focus God whom we cannot see. This is not so easy to do with brothers. They will not allow us to treat them in that way. When faced with the blunt truth, nobody can keep his illusions for long.

Most communities start with a honeymoon. A set of egoisms coincide, we scrutinize these together for a long time and we call this brotherly love. (That's the worst egoism of all — enthusiasm for our own charity.) But if we continue to share our brotherly life in common, the spell is soon broken. Then there begins the true work of love by which we slowly learn to overcome every disappointment, every discouragement, every humiliation, every repugnance.

"If any man say, I love God, and hateth his brother; he is a liar. For he that loveth not his brother whom he seeth, how can he love God whom he seeth not?"[3] To love our brothers freely, without reciprocation, often to receive ingratitude and indifference in return, to see others use our friendship as a springboard to betray us, to see others use our gift without realizing that we are now impoverished, is to share the fate of God. This is how God loves us.

"We know that we have passed from death to life, because we love the brethren",[4] says St. John again. No one can escape from this communion. A contemplative is one who communes with others at the level which is deepest, absolute, and also most painful. At the very level of his being, at God's level. We enter a Trappist monastery to be closer to all our brothers, not in order to say "Our Father" all on our own. Anyone who withdrew into a cloister to be all alone with God, would be a pagan. "By this shall all men know that you are my disciples, if you have love one for another."[5]

St. Paul wrote to the Corinthians: "You come together, not for the better, but for the worse. For first of all I hear that when you come together in the church, there are schisms among you . . . When you come therefore together into one place, it is not now to eat the Lord's supper. For everyone taketh before his own supper to eat. And one indeed is hungry and another is drunk."[6]

"I hear. . .that there are schisms among you. . ." Nowadays there is nothing but schisms. We don't even speak

[3] 1 John 4:20. [4] 1 John 3:14. [5] John 13:35.
[6] 1 Cor. 11:17-18, 20-21.

to each other any longer, we hardly look at each other and we all see nothing wrong in this. Wouldn't St. Paul be wild!

The first Christians began with a brotherly meal. They shared and then they took communion. And the scandal was that "one was drunk and another hungry". We have found a remedy for this disgraceful state of affairs; this question of a meal is settled exclusively at home. Thus there is no longer any scandal. We get drunk behind closed doors. We are hungry privately, at home. And no embarrassment need disturb any longer the smooth unfolding of the communion service. "Painless communion." Everything happens quietly, as in well-organized dental surgeries. The pain begins only when we have got home. *Ite missa est! Pax vobis!* Everyone manages to pretend that his neighbour is in peace. "And if a brother or sister", wrote the apostle James, "be naked, and want daily food: And one of you say to them: Go in peace, be you warmed and filled; yet give them not those things that are necessary for the body, what shall it profit?"[7]

It is shocking to think how inured we have become to living in a world of fiction. We need cataclysms to discover the distance between what we pretend to be and what we are. Thus at school during the war we used to have at regular hours the semblance of a meal, a truly brotherly meal. Having swallowed the official rations together — in communion — we used to withdraw as if nothing had happened. When we had returned to our rooms, we would go to a carefully locked drawer, and each one of us would take out his own personal store of food and have a really good meal according to his resources. Then one day an unforeseen event upset the whole arrangement. The school

[7] James 2:15-16.

was requisitioned; we had to take refuge in a neighbouring country house and there we could no longer have our own rooms. We were all housed together in a few large rooms turned into dormitories. There was general consternation. For the first few days, each one of us, before his open cupboard — like a horse in its box — stealthily, with his back turned, attempted to continue, to maintain his own private communion. But the uneasiness grew from day to day. Then, with great reluctance, one after the other, we disclosed our stocks. We owned up to what we had; we agreed to admit that we had more than our neighbour. We agreed to remove this inequality; we agreed to share, to put everything in common. We learnt, we discovered the meaning of communion.

For many years we had "been to communion" every morning. And we had never experienced pooling things in common. For ten, twelve years we had taken communion and for the first time we were sharing.

When, some months later, we went back to our school and to our rooms and it became possible for us to take on our old habits again, we could no longer bear the idea of going back to our individualism. Having, in spite of ourselves, learnt the taste of brotherhood, we could no longer forget it. We no longer wanted to go back to our lonely comfort, the dreariness of which we had since discovered. To the very end, our daily communion lasted from morning to night.

When shall we share for the first time? We perform all the rites of sharing, all the signs of brotherhood, all the ceremonies of communion. But these rites become for us a substitute for truth instead of leading us there. We shall be no nearer to God than we are to each one of our brothers. We share as much with God as we do with our broth-

17

ers. What a miserable share! When shall we stop lying? When shall we rid ourselves of our illusions?

The danger of such a lie explains the harshness of St. Peter towards Ananias and Saphira.[8] If their story causes us no loss of sleep, it is because we no longer even understand the meaning of the words we read. Or we have come to behave as if the demands of Christianity do not concern us. What had Ananias and Saphira done, after all? Because they were Christians they had sold all their possessions. That was really not so bad to start with! And they had come to pay the proceeds to the apostles, "keeping back part of it". They had put by for themselves a small pear to quench their thirst; and they had not said so. And for this imperfection, this very human act of prudence, Peter actually destroyed them.

It was because "the multitude of believers had but one heart and one soul. Neither did anyone say that aught of the things which he possessed was his own; but all things were common unto them."[9] This life in common was not a sort of new custom they were trying to establish, a new way of life that they were attempting to launch, but the sign of a true love, as when compatriots meet abroad and help each other, delighted to know that they come from the same far-distant fatherland, a fatherland where the rule is to love one another.

We now understand why Peter could not endure those people who cheated, who concealed, who held back. "Ananias, why hath Satan tempted thy heart, that thou shouldst lie to the Holy Ghost and by fraud keep part of the price of the land. Whilst it remained, did it not remain to thee? And after it was sold, was it not in thy power? Why

[8] Acts 5:1-11.   [9] Acts 4:32.

hast thou conceived this thing in thy heart?" Why are you playing the fool? Why do you talk of communion, when you have decided to go it alone? Why do you pretend to commune when you want to keep your little business and your little secrets all to yourself? Every man for himself? All right, then. But at least don't lie. "Thou hast not lied to men, but to God."[10] Your relations with God are the same as those with your fellows. Your attitude towards others is a startling revelation of the sincerity of your love for God.

We cannot tolerate anyone who tries to prevent us from withdrawing into ourselves. In our Church, it is those who would suggest sharing who would be destroyed! The assembly of Christians has unfortunately been moulded on a caste society. Frozen though it is, it looks as if it is gently beginning to thaw. Are we amongst those who with all their heart, with all their might, are hastening its return to communion, to the love of the early days?

At Caesarea, Peter asked: "Can any man forbid water, that these should not be baptized, who have received the Holy Ghost as well as we?"[11] The Holy Ghost is the spirit of love. When we look at certain "pagans" of our times who seem to have a far greater spirit of charity towards their neighbour than many of us, should we not think of these words of Peter? Have we had our Pentecost? Have we realized what happened? Did we receive that Spirit when he was given to us? Pentecost is the destruction of the Tower of Babel. At Pentecost they all heard each other, they all understood each other. They all heard their own tongue spoken.

The clearest sign of original sin is a collective one; it is

[10] Acts 5:3-4.   [11] Acts 10:47.

the breakdown of communion, of understanding. It is the absence of love, the absence of brotherhood, which is restored, set up again by the redemption.

"That he might make known unto us the mystery of his will . . . to re-establish all things in Christ . . . in him . . . in whom you also, after you had heard the word of truth (the gospel of your salvation) in whom also believing, you were signed with the holy Spirit of promise."[12] All those who, at Pentecost, experienced that miraculous unity, that unparalleled moment of communion, could not imagine living otherwise. (Have we not sometimes felt that ourselves? Have we been true to this revelation made to us?) From the moment the disciples were baptized in the Holy Spirit, in the spirit of unity — in the spirit of brotherly communion — they would have looked upon an individualistic, profane life, as a sacrilege. Because it is a sacrilege, when we share a life which is a gift, to disfigure it by our refusal. Does an individualistic life seem profane to us? Have we grasped the essential thing? Have we learnt to say, *Our* Father?

St. John Chrysostom always hoped that he would see his flock (the Christians of Constantinople) go back to the community life of the early days. This is what he wrote to them: "In monasteries they live as in the primitive Church. Well, who ever died of hunger there? Who has not found abundant nourishment there? Nevertheless men today are more afraid of living this way than of falling into the sea. Why have we not tried it? We would fear it less. What a grace it is! If a handful of faithful — they were scarcely eight thousand — without waiting for a reward, dared, in the face of the universe where they had only enemies,

[12] Eph. 1:9-13.

20

make a brave effort at life in common, how many more could do it now that there are faithful all over the world? Would there be a single pagan left? Not one. We would attract them all. We would win them all . . ."[13]

This is an inspiration that has visited all those who are attentive to the Spirit of God. In every age of the world, in every generation of the Church, the Spirit has inspired, in one form or another, that wish to share and to commune, to live as a poor man amongst the poor, so as to have the same wealth as they have and to be able to say: "Our Father."

[13] *Homily on the Acts.*

Father

How DO you picture God? What image, what feeling does he evoke in you? By what name do you call him? Is it "Father"?

The Son came to reveal the Father to us. And all that most Christians have retained of his mission is the revelation of the Son. Their religion miscarries. They remain on the way ("I am the way") instead of going where he is leading them. All their love of Christ should lead towards the Father. They would never be nearer to Jesus, more united to him, than by becoming sons. They would never show him more love and honour than when urged by his bidding and schooled by his divine teaching, they would make bold to say, Father.

And yet, for many of them, the fact of having found the Son, of having become attached to the Son, releases them from all obligations towards the Father. In the eyes of men, they want to be sons without being brothers. In the eyes of God, they want to be brothers without being sons. Christ's complaint remains true: "Just Father, the world hath not known thee."[1]

Who amongst us thinks of God as a Father? Or at

[1] John 17:25.

22

least — for not everyone has had a father who was a revelation of God—who wonders what he would be like as a father, as a mother, and believes that God would be even better than that? We are rather inclined to believe the opposite; we are good fathers, good mothers, and God is a little like us.

We reach the stage where the majority of Christians would not care to be the God they picture. They would be an improvement on him. Voltaire made the terrible comment: "God made man to his image and likeness, but man has returned the compliment." Man is naturally idolatrous; he is for ever making a God to his own image. Each one of us is tempted to imagine a distant God, vaguely dissatisfied, indifferent, absent-minded, spiteful, grumbling. As we do not love him very much, we presume that he cannot be very fond of us.

But Revelation tells us precisely that God is not like us, and that in order to discover what his feelings are for us, we must not consult our feelings for him; that God is Father, that God is love, and that he loves us without our loving him, and that he loved us first.

We say "Our Father"; but how often have we believed it? "Faith relates, not to the statement of dogma, but to the reality which it expresses" said St. Thomas. Only too rarely do we seize the truth of what is usually for us a worn-out word.

What an absence of faith, what a lack of trust in him this is! We rely on him with our lips, not with our heart. What would we say if our children thought they were being left to their own devices, that they were being abandoned by us and they did not expect from us everything that they needed.

Among all the influences that contribute to our development, none is more important than our idea of God. If this idea is lifeless, vague, cold, our religion will be the same, a deism, a form of loneliness. And this idea is all the more important because we become like the God we picture. The whole history of humanity has been corrupted, has been broken, because Adam conceived a false notion of God. He wanted to be like God. I hope you have never thought that *this* was Adam's sin; what other ambition could he have? And is this not exactly what God had asked him to do? Adam simply chose the wrong model. He thought that God was an independent, self-sufficient being, and in order to become like him, he rebelled and disobeyed.

But when God revealed himself, when God wished to show what he was really like, he revealed that he was love, tenderness, effusion of himself, infinite kindness towards others, affection, subordination. God revealed himself to be obedient, obedient unto death. Whilst believing that he was becoming God, Adam became totally different from him. He entrenched himself in solitude, and God was but communion.

Each one of us commits the error and the mistake that Adam made. Where is it that you expect to find happiness? Surely by becoming richer and richer, more and more independent, more and more free from all bondage, by doing what you want to do, by thinking what pleases you, by providing for the future, by relying on your fortune? Alas, this is the very opposite of the Our Father.

Whereas if your ambition is to love more and more, to be affectionate, to be meek, to delight in making others rejoice, to find wealth in giving, to discover strength in serving, to be kind to others, then you become like the Father. Then indeed you become a son.

24

We are always tempted by the devil — the damned one, the one who is apart, the one who is cut off. We are always under the impression that we are superior, that we exist more fully when we possess, when we enjoy, than when we give ourselves, when we are independent than when we are dependent, when we are free than when we are subject. We always have a tendency to harden, to assert ourselves. The stronger we are, the more we tend to be self-sufficient, to organize ourselves, to impose ourselves on others, to be something on our own account, for ourselves.

God does not live alone. He exists only in relation. He needed to be several to be God. He needed to be several to be love. He needed to be several to be gift. The Father is only father by generating the Son. The Son is only son by giving himself back to his Father, by becoming in turn a gift. God has revealed that he is not a lonely God, "the eternal bachelor of the universe", the infinite egoist. God is effusion, ecstasy, communication, absolute gift of self. Every Sunday, in the Preface of the Holy Trinity, we rejoice when we sing: *"Non in unius singularitate personae..."* How lucky it is that you are not lonely, how lucky it is that you are several, what a joy it is that you are love, that you are Father! It is being Father that gives him the wish to create. He would not have created us if he had not had a Son. And he has created us to the image of the latter. He has become our Father.

What does it mean to be a Father?

To be a Father is an initiative of love. To be a Father is to give oneself, it is to love someone before he loves you, when he does not yet love you, when he does not yet exist. It is to love someone gratuitously, without his having done anything for one. "It is hard enough to find

25

anyone who will die on behalf of a just man, although there may be those who will face death for one so deserving. But here, as if God meant to prove how well he loves us, it was while we were still sinners that Christ, in his own appointed time, died for us."[2]

When we bring a child into the world, what guarantee have we that he will be happy, generous, grateful, loving, upright? One only: I will love him so much, I will bear with him so patiently, I will forgive him so often that the day will come when he will love me as I love him.

This is the only guarantee that God has got as far as we are concerned. Those who truly love us do not love us on account of the qualities which they discover in us when they begin to love us, but on account of the goodness of their own heart, which is so strong, so just, so faithful, that they feel sure that one day they will awaken in us a love like theirs. Love alone is a creator, only the wild generosity of love is capable of generating life.

Watch two adults, two fully developed creatures, bending down with absolute devotion over a little one, subjecting themselves passionately to him, attributing an infinite value to him, ready to give their blood, their fortune, their life for him, for the insignificant and unknown little being who, as yet, hardly exists. And thanks to their prodigality, the child is born, survives, smiles, finds without difficulty the normal conditions of its existence, and awakens one day to the love that has created it.

When a child reaches fifteen or sixteen years of age, it often bewilders its parents, and they no longer recognize the creature they loved. Alas, it is often too the age when

[2] Rom. 5:7-9.

they think they know it, when they judge it. We should say: "This is the age when they no longer love it." And therefore when they cease to create it. For to love a creature is to believe, is to hope in it for ever. Those parents who no longer believe in the infinite possibilities for good enclosed within the hearts of their children, those parents do not love them any longer, they no longer have sufficient faith and courage to love them. Then the children look abroad; they look around them for a girl or a boy friend, a master, someone who will again believe in them and will enable them to grow. For we only grow well for those by whom we are loved. We are grateful to a person who loves us because he has believed sufficiently in us to enable us to dare be with him so much better, so much more affectionate, so much more vulnerable, more generous than we would have been with anyone else.

To love another is to make to him the most powerful, the most imperious of all calls; it stirs up within him a hidden silent being who cannot avoid responding to our call, a being so novel that even he who bore it did not know it and which is yet so genuine that he cannot help recognizing it, although he is seeing it for the first time. It is thus that God loves us, loyally and with infinite patience, because he is infinitely Father. God can be denied, forgotten. He cannot deny or forget us. Man may be without God; God cannot be without man. Man may cease being a son, but God cannot cease being a Father.

God has created out of love, to give and to give himself, to quicken other beings with his life, to rejoice other beings with his joy, so that there should exist creatures to be loved and loaded with gifts, creatures that should know the joy of living and loving. For he is

27

so much a Father that he wants to give us everything. He wants us to know everything about him. He has therefore given us the power of giving, of being ourselves fathers. He has given us the love of giving so that we should experience the joy of God. He has given us so much that he has given us the power to give.

But the catechism says that God has created the world for his own glory. If he makes everything for himself, has he therefore become again the infinite egoist? What is the glory of God? God loves. His glory is to be Son, to be love, to love us as much as that. God has created the world out of love, so as to manifest his love, so that his creatures should know how, to what extent, God knows how to love.

For us, therefore, to learn how to become Father, is to become God. Becoming a father helps us understand what it means to be God. It means learning how to awaken life; but not only physical life, of course. That alone would indeed be a miserable form of fatherhood. True spiritual fatherhood, which exceeds beyond measure the fatherhood of nature, awakens the soul to faith, trust, truth, love, and joy. How many children are orphans from the very moment they are born; there is no one to awaken them to any other life but that of the body and of tears! When, in the Old Testament a remarkable being was needed, he was born of a sterile woman, for true fecundity comes from God. And in the New Testament, he was born of a Virgin.

God is solely Father. We are fathers to some extent. We belong to our children, of course, but we are tied up with so many other things as well, our business, our profession, our marriage, our tastes, our achievements, our amusements — and we also belong to ourselves. We are not fatherly enough. It is God alone who is perfectly a Father. "And no one knoweth the Son but the Father." [3] He gives himself utterly to his Son. There is not an atom of selfishness or self-seeking in him. That is why he has a perfect Son who is perfectly like him.

Jesus said: "And all my things are thine." And he added, "And thine are mine". [4] For what are the things of the Father? He loves. He gives himself. Therefore what the Son has received is to surrender himself. His own devotion to the Father is but another revelation of the way the Father loves him. From whom did he learn so much love? From his Father: "The Son cannot do anything of himself, but what he seeth the Father doing." [5]

God is indeed the most daring of all beings. He has placed all his happiness in his love. He makes all his happiness depend on another in whom he is well pleased. The Father does not know himself well. The Father does not love himself well, he only knows himself, he only loves himself through his Son, who is his only true image, the radiation of his glory, the stamp of his substance. For this reason the Father glorifies himself. He never speaks of himself when he manifests himself in the theophanies of the New Testament. He shows us his Son and he says to us: "This is my beloved Son in whom I am well pleased." [6] In him I am more myself than in myself.

Why does a mother answer, "Jack is well, Frank is this, Peter is that" when we ask her news of herself? Because her children are what is most alive in her, henceforth her life lies there, it is they that matter for her. It was quite natural for her to forget herself. She is pleased in others. The Father is he who is well pleased in another. It

[3] Matt. 11:27.   [4] John 17:10.   [5] John 5:19.   [6] Matt. 17:5.

is the Father who reveals himself in the Son. We must ask the Son to show us the Father: "Lord, show us the Father . . ."

Through a deplorable misunderstanding, many Christians still picture the redemption as a debate between the Father and the Son, the Son intervening in order to appease the anger of the Father. (In an appeal for a pilgrimage to the Sacred Heart we read, "The Sacred Heart of Jesus is the only defence that can protect us against the anger of the Father . . .")

Now Revelation tells us that God so loved the world that he gave his only-begotten Son to save it. Could any step have cost him more? Could any gesture have required greater love? "For God indeed was in Christ reconciling the world to himself."[7] "I say not to you that I will ask the Father for you, for the Father himself loveth you."[8]

Many believe that the initiative of our salvation came from the Son. But the Gospel says: "For I came not of myself; but he sent me."[9] "The words that I speak to you, I speak not of myself. But the Father who abideth in me, he doth the works."[10] Jesus is revelation of the Father. He has told us that the Father was entirely in the Son, that those who saw the Son saw him, and that all the love that the Son gave us came from him. "He that seeth me seeth the Father also."[11] Have you ever meditated on these words before Jesus crucified?

Jesus came to help us know the Father. Jesus died revealing to us the love of the Father. And we have only seen in this a kind of protective intervention, a sort of protest, a divorce in the very bosom of the Trinity,

---

[7] 2 Cor. 5:19.   [8] John 16:26-27.   [9] John 8:42.
[10] John 14:10.   [11] John 14:9.

30

which is love. It is as if we had seen the gesture of Christ without understanding the meaning which he has explained to us, which he has never ceased to explain to us.

When we read the beginning of the Gospel of St. John, we brighten up at the words, "And the Word was made flesh and dwelt among us." This concerns us. We have held him. But do we even know how the text goes on? "And we saw his glory . . ." Glory has become a hollow word for us because we no longer know what it means. Glory is love. It is God who communicates himself to us; his presence which becomes more and more intimate, "And we saw his glory, the glory as it were of the only begotten of the Father."

Before dying, Jesus said the same thing again: "I have finished the work which thou gavest me to do . . . I have manifested thy name to the men . . . Now they have known that all things which thou hast given me are from thee."[12]

This is the essential dogma. The Father sent the Son "because the words which thou gavest me, I have given to them . . . and they have believed that thou didst send me".[13] Have we really believed it? If we did believe it, would it not illuminate our life?

[12] John 17:4, 6, 7.   [13] John 17:8.

Who art in Heaven

"For as the heavens are exalted above the earth, so are my ways exalted above your ways, and my thoughts above your thoughts."

(Isa. 55:9)

CHRISTIAN prayer differs radically from pagan prayer, natural prayer. It is as unlike it as Christian baptism is unlike Jewish baptism. The latter is a mere gesture, a rite, a symbol, a sign of purification. Christian baptism purifies with an efficacy which comes from Above, with truly divine force. In the same way, prayer as instituted for Christians comes from Above, it is an act of God. To show that the two prayers were entirely different, Jesus said to his disciples: "If you ask the Father anything in my name, he will give it you"; "Hitherto you have not asked anything in my name."[1]

There are two prayers, two quite different religions, yet I imagine that many Christians say the supernatural prayer as if it belonged to natural religion.

Pagan religion consists essentially in what man does for God. God is the blessed and motionless centre of all our endeavours. Wretched humanity crawls towards him to steal from him a little of his light and warmth. Only the most skilful, the cleverest, the strongest will succeed.

[1] John 16:23-24.

32

There is something great about this religion, since it is the desperate effort of man in his search for God, but it is grievous, poor, laborious, exceptional, and, like all human endeavour, it is a mixture of nobility and ignominy, generosity and calculation, love and cruelty.

But supernatural religion does not consist in those poor, feeble, wretched things that we do for God. It consists in those wonders of generosity, love, and forgiveness which God does for us. What is true in natural religion is the basis of the truth of our own religion. You are quite right to search for God, to love him, and to want him. But you are even more right than you think, because he is infinitely better than you had imagined. God is so good that it is he who comes to us, who searches for us, who gives himself to us, who loves us. We Christians are not better than the rest; but our God is better than us. True religion consists in marvelling, in falling into ecstasy before the great things that God does, despite the weakness and the meanness of his servants. God causes us to love him, God causes us to know him, God causes us to pray to him.

We continually forget that we are not Christians because we love God; we are Christians because we believe that God loves us. The saints are those who believe that God loves them: "And we have known and have believed the charity which God hath to us."[2] And it is a difficult thing to do, because we are unworthy of it, and it is humiliating to be loved without having deserved it. It is difficult to believe in something which is inexplicable. However, we must not search for explanations. A thousand arguments do not produce a shred of evidence. But

[2] 1 John 4:16.

when we love, a thousand objections do not produce a single doubt.

Pagan prayer is a wager, a piece of folly. It would be a kind of blasphemy were it not a sign, a signal, a foreboding that God will come to fulfil and grant our wishes. It claims to inform God, to tell him about a state of affairs to which he does not attach sufficient importance. Even better than this, it undertakes to stimulate a God who is asleep, to move a God who is indifferent, to improve a God who is imperfect. And it improves him according to our lights. Each one of us knows very well what he would do if he were God. Each one of us has a plan, or at least a suggestion which we are ready to submit to him, if he were only willing to listen to reason. We don't trust God's ideas very much. At heart, who amongst us does not believe that he would direct our fate a good deal better if he were God; things would run differently, they would be far better organized and we would do things far better. Lord, do now for me what I would do for you if you were me and if I were God. Have we never carried this same blasphemy, unspoken, deep down in our heart? Who is it amongst us who has not been tempted a little to move the heart of God? To stir his inertia? To direct a little his activity, to disturb a little his inactivity?

Would it not be true to say that our Our Father, the one which would reflect the most secret and natural tendency of our heart, would be this: "Our Father, remain in heaven, hallowed be my name (who does not wish that his name were better known, esteemed, at least that of our family, our convent, our brotherhood), our kingdom come (may our brotherhoods extend, may people understand that a promising revival is taking place, to which it would be foolish of them not to rally; may they know a little how much good all this is doing etc.), and above all may our will be done (one never knows what yours has in store for us, whereas we are always safe with ours). And forgive us our trespasses as we . . . Do try to be as unspiteful as we are, see how good and magnanimous we are in spite of our churlish looks, and try a little to do likewise. Make an effort, be as good as we are."

The cult of idols is not a platitude of the sermons of twenty centuries ago; it is a permanent temptation, an article in current production, manufactured daily. Our prayers are insidious. They try and enlist God in our service. And the supreme service which he can render us will be to enable us to do one day without him.

For many people God is the chemist-shop God (first-aid kit with emergency remedies; but when the holidays went well, there was no need to open it), the parachute-God (to be opened at the last minute, but we hope not to get into that state), the fire-extinguisher God ("In case of fire, break the glass", after the fire is over to be put back in its place with a brand-new glass). Finally, God is sometimes of great use to us as an undertaker's prop. Suddenly at a funeral everyone talks of God, of heaven... "I will pray for you", "He is happy up there", "God has taken him back." Everything is trotted out. An hour later, of course, these dismal ideas have been cast aside.

For if the purpose of God is to sanctify us, to mend us, to protect us, if he is the agent and the instrument of our moral build-up, he naturally becomes useless the moment the structure has been built. This is the unexpressed hope of many of our prayers: "Give me that and then I will leave you alone", "Give me my share of inheritance and I will flee far from you." Most people who go to confession, confess mainly in order not to go to confession again. Some people reason like this: either confession serves no purpose whatever, in which case I can excuse myself from it, or else it serves some purpose, in which case I ought not to sin again. "Although I pray, although I go to confession, I still sin. It's all useless. I pray no longer." Who has not talked like this?

But God, of course, never promised that we should sin no longer. (If he had, he would no longer have the joy of forgiving us). God has promised always to forgive us. "Go, say that sins are forgiven"; these are the good tidings — not suppressed, *forgiven*. We shall still commit many sins and much will be forgiven us, and in being continually forgiven, we will learn much love. He to whom little is forgiven, loves only a little.

The prime purpose of confession is not to ensure our moral infallibility. It reveals to us the love and the generosity of the Father in forgiving us: "God who displayeth thy almighty power chiefly by showing mercy and forbearance . . ."[3] We will never be able to learn enough about the goodness of the Father. The essential thing is not no longer to sin, but to love, to have learnt his love. You will go to heaven because you will be pleased with God and not because you are pleased with yourself. The worst enemy of God is the wish to do without him; the worst sin against God is perhaps the wish to sin no longer ("because I dislike sin") so as to have no need to have recourse to him. That is pride. Pride does not consist in having too good an idea of ourselves — that is a tame and harmless form of vanity. Pride means refusing to be dependent on another, sheltering in a desperate wish to be

[3] Prayer on the Sunday after Pentecost.

self-sufficient and relying on our own strength. It means preferring to be unhappy, provided we are all alone.

To pray means surrendering ourselves. It means saying to God: "Work on me. I place my trust in Thee." Adam was unable to show such trust. He wanted to control, to take a hand, to free himself, to be himself. But Jesus said: "Father, into thy hands I commend my spirit."

This insane wish to do without God, necessarily leads us to doubt and unbelief. God cannot fulfil our wishes, load us with gifts, free us, settle us on this earth. It is in heaven that he is our Father. Let us not, therefore, criticize him, hate him, revolt against him because he refuses to do our will.

All this religion—our religious emotions, our sentimental or selfish devotions—are an exaltation of our own self, not an encounter with him. He should grow and we should diminish. The pagan god is an idol. We must lose our faith in that God in order to recover the real faith. And we must give up the hope of receiving his favours. Because our God—the true God—never ceases to disappoint the miserable hopes measured by our standards, to which we cautiously limit our ambitions, in order to offer us a hope measured by his own standards. He calls us to a state which is his, to enable us to pass from our world to his... "My Kingdom is not of this world." "Our Father . . . who art in heaven!"

Supernatural prayer is filial prayer; it is said in the name of Jesus, that is to say in the name of the Son. It is an inspired prayer that comes from above. To pray "in the name of the Son" does not mean saying at the end of our prayer, as we hurry a little because we know the way it goes but we have to say because it sets the whole thing in motion: "Through Jesus Christ your Son, our Lord, who liveth and reigneth ... etc." To pray in the name of Jesus means to pray with the Spirit of Jesus, the Spirit within us which cries out, "Abba, Father".[4] Christian prayer is the one where God himself prays within us, where we give ourselves to him, where we allow him to lead us.

Because it is God who prays within us, it is the Holy Ghost who says: "Father, our Father." "The Spirit also helpeth our infirmity. For we know not what we should pray for as we ought; but the Spirit himself asketh for us with unspeakable groanings."[5] God prays within us, God manifests himself within us.

Prayer is the opposite of pride. To pray is to let in things which do not depend on us, to trust another, to rely on someone greater than ourselves, to become again son and daughter: "Hitherto you have asked for nothing in my name." Prayer comes from above; like every best gift and every perfect grace, it comes down from the Father of lights.[6] Many have fallen back into paganism to such an extent that they have come to believe that prayer is a purely human activity, a call to God, a speech made to God. Above all things it is an action of God within us. In our prayer we must not make the mistake of Chanticleer who thought his song caused the sun to rise. He thought that it awoke on hearing his voice, and that should one day Chanticleer by accident fail to crow, the sun, just imagine it, would not rise! Reality is far more beautiful than Chanticleer imagined. It was the sun which, with the softest ray of dawn, came to awaken Chanticleer. He was only the herald of all the light, warmth, and kindness contained within the universe.

[4] Rom. 8:15.   [5] Rom. 8:26.   [6] Cf. James 1:17.

When we come to pray, let us cry with happiness, let us laugh with joy. God is at work! God is active within us. God has already succeeded in lessening the resistance which we continually oppose to him. He has already obtained his first victory over us, the incredible gesture that we should have begun to pray. And now if we remain, if we wait long enough, we are going to know, we are going to learn how he has already fulfilled our wishes.

This prayer is an uprooting — "who art in heaven". It removes us from ourselves to take us into God. It lets God become God within us. It consents to allow itself to be lifted towards heaven, instead of attempting to attract God to earth. We must beware of our will, which, as Simone Weil has said, destroys the balance by forcing the beam. If we want to restore the balance, we must do so by altering patiently the load of the scales so that ours, which is always overloaded, should become lighter and God's by becoming heavier, should prevail. A real miracle is required to lift that mountain of cares, weariness, and revolt which weighs down our scales.

But prayer works miracles and lifts mountains. When we have said "Father" we have already said everything. We have finished. We know what will follow. Once more, it will cost us a great deal. If we believe that he is Father, then we are already defenceless. If all that is thine is mine, then, what can I say except: "Whatever is mine is thine."

Whatever is thine . . .? This means being gift all the time, being no longer anything but gift ("Oh, if you knew the gift of God!"), being for ever dependent on another, being for ever turned, stretched, drawn (crucified) towards another. Are we capable of consenting to join in this terrible, this divine game? Every day in the *Veni Creator* we say: *"Per Te sciamus da Patrem"*, "May we know the

39

Father, may we become sons ..." We are the heirs of God; yes, but what does that mean? What do we inherit? God can only love and give. He has nothing else; therefore he has nothing else to give us. What will we receive from him? The capacity to give. As sons and heirs we will have the privilege of carrying on the activities of one who does nothing but give, give himself. That is why so many people prefer to give up that inheritance. That is why we so rarely dare say, Father.

To say: "Our Father who art in heaven", means consenting to be a son with the Son, to be a son like the Son, to be converted into a son: "For what things soever the Father doth, these the Son also doth in like manner."[7] Of course it hurts. Of course it is exhausting. Having said the Our Father, it is normal for us to be drained, quite literally emptied of ourselves.

But by what aberration of mind do we look on this as a loss? How is it that we don't know that it is only then that something can start? Why do we not think: Father, if you are Father, all will be well. If you are Father, all is in your hands. If you are Father, if you are my Father, I am no longer afraid. I am confident. It will look terrible, but I know that nothing that is not desirable or preferable will happen. If you lead, we cannot be wrong. I love what you want, I want what you desire.

The prayers of the days before Jesus, pagan prayers, are a pathetic attempt to approach with our poor human means a mysterious power to which it seems we must make some indeterminate sacrifice. But it is disheartening. We rebel all the time: "All that I have done for God! All that I have given up for the sake of religion! To think of the

---

[7] John 5:19.

things I could have enjoyed — if I had not thought that all these sacrifices would be of some use. And what have I received from all this?" To consent to believe and to pray knowing that God is going to be of no "use" to us is the only reply to such a revolt. It is we who must serve God. We must go to him, not to be satisfied but to be sacrificed, and sacrificed means to be made sacred.

No one can see God and live; so the first thing he will do if we approach him is to make us die to our own ideas, to our own ambitions — even our spiritual ones — to our plans — even if they are edifying ones — to our merits, to all those pious combinations which we used to place as a screen between him and ourselves. As soon as we have understood this, as soon as this upheaval has taken place we shall find peace. Before that, we are like a man who walks against the stream of a procession: everyone knocks him, hits him, pushes him. Everything hurts him. Yet no one has a grudge against him. He has but to turn round on his heels and everything which used to hurt him will now surround, carry, and lift him.

Supernatural prayer can say to natural prayer, to pagan prayer, what Jesus said to the Jews: "You are from beneath, I am from above. You are of this world: I am not of this world."[8] You have believed that I have come from the Father. Pray in my name, pray as I pray, go where I go. I am leaving the world and I am going to the Father. I share the interests of the Father, the views of the Father, the loves of the Father — who so loved the world that he sent his Son. It is the Father's pleasure — and you should desire it — that you should be happy. The Father's life — and you should choose it — that you should live. "Now this

[8] John 8:23.

is eternal life: that they may know thee, the only true God, and Jesus Christ, whom thou hast sent . . . Father, that the world may know that thou hast sent me and hast loved them, as thou hast also loved me."[9]

Religion does not consist in what we do for God, but in those incredible things which God does for us: the Incarnation, the Crucifixion, the Resurrection, Pentecost — the effusion of God over us — Prayer — Mass — Communion — God who offers himself to us, God who communicates himself to us in all manner of means.

It matters little whether prayer bores us. Let us do it because it delights God, because he asks us for it. Let us join him where he has preceded us. God is happy to see us near him; he loves to give to us. We must believe it. Who then will not adore with enthusiasm? Who, if he believed it, would not go to rejoice the heart of God by submitting to his love?

Prayer "serves" to detach us from ourselves in order to attach ourselves to him, to die to our own life in order to receive his, to forget our own way of praying in order to learn his; then we will be fulfilled. Praying like Jesus, we will be fulfilled—like Jesus. "Hitherto you have not asked anything in my name... If you ask the Father anything in my name, he will give it you";[10] but a little later he adds: "Again I leave the world and I go to the Father."[11] To want what the Son wants: the Father. To ask for what the Son asks: the Father's kingdom. That prayer is always granted: "What you ask for in my name."

Have we ever realized the responsibility which this

[9] John 17:3, 23.
[10] John 16:24, 23.
[11] John 16:28.

implies? We have been entrusted with a liturgical, a priestly function. If we pray, we will cause the kingdom to come, we will make the name hallowed, we will bring back sons to the Father, we will do his will. Every time we are unfaithful to this prayer, we delay his advent.

Hallowed be thy Name

SURELY this is typical of the kind of request that has no meaning — a sort of religious parrot-cry. God *is* holy; "He alone is holy! He alone is Lord!" How could he be more hallowed than he is already? And by us of all people! It would not be quite so bad if we said, "May we be hallowed", but not God. And what are we thinking of when we ask that the name be hallowed? Have we ever thought about anything?

Christ has done nothing greater than to reveal to us the name of God. To Moses in the burning bush, God replied, "I am who am." Is this a metaphysical description or a wish to go no further? "I am who am. Don't ask any more." Whatever it was, it was mysterious, and the Jews were already so fearful of the name that they often replaced it by a series of circumlocutions, for fear of evoking the oppressive presence of God.

Amongst the ancients, to name was to call. Whoever named had power over the one he named. (Hence the greatest of all forms of treason was to betray the names of the gods to the enemy.) When Adam in Paradise took charge of the animals, he named them. Jesus gave us the Father, when he gave us his name. "The Father himself loves you." God loves us; this is no formula. What does it mean? It means that we have power over him.

We have power over those who love us. Children, weak though they are, know this — and they sulk and refuse to eat, because it is the way they lead their parents. It is a topsy-turvy way of proving to their parents that they know that they are loved, that they are considered important. We are important for those who love us. God loves us.

Only too often we are discouraged in our love for God. We do indeed give him a little of our time. But we are so much under the impression that it adds nothing to him, that he could well do without it. What a joy it would be if we managed to find out that our love has a meaning for him whom we love; if we came to believe that it would matter to him if we thought about him, if he could not do without it. Would it not be sufficient to brighten, to re-kindle, rejoice our whole life?

So God is not independent, invulnerable? Are we independent of our children? Does our happiness not depend on their joy? We are infinitely dependent on those who depend on us. Is there such a thing as an insensitive love? Let us not call it love.

To be a father means precisely to suffer. To become a father means to become vulnerable. The strong creature who loves a weak one places his happiness at the mercy of the weakling. To love a person means inevitably to depend on him, it means giving him power over us. By loving us of his own free will, God has chosen to give us power over him.

On plates from Normandy, one can read this cruel and cynical phrase: "It is always the one who loves least who is the strongest." It is always the one who is least in love who leads the other. In his dealings with us, God will always be the weakest, because he loves the most.

Man rebelling against God is the bird which dashes against the cliff in the storm. But God in his mercy became flesh so that he and not we should bear the fury of the impact. We are of the race of Jacob, we are the real Israel that wrestles all night with the angel and that deserves his name: "Strong against God".[1]

Then . . . God needs men? Strictly speaking, no. God wanted to need men. Whilst men themselves never cease to dream dimly of the day when they will no longer need anyone, like those young men that want to be "tough". Yes, they want to be loved but they do not want to love, they do not want to be sensitive because it hurts too much. God on the other hand suffers. Is not our religion that of a crucified God?

The ideal of the adolescent is to be screened, protected, covered with armour plate, to be insensitive so that others should not hurt him too much. This withdrawal, this isolation to prevent us from suffering too much is a deep and everlasting tendency of man. The adolescent likes to be loved, to receive. It is the adult who loves without requiring any return, who loves unconditionally. This is what is meant by reaching the adult state; to become a father, to become a mother, to become capable of a love like that — and we remain children so long as we prefer to receive rather than to give, so long as we prefer to be loved rather than to love. The adolescent's ideal is to be appreciated, to have successes whilst remaining nobly (he thinks!) indifferent, insensible, invulnerable; until the day comes, years later, when he realizes that he could really

[1] Gen. 32:28.

love someone, that he could love someone so much that he could give it all up, so much that he could accept being vulnerable to someone, being sensitive to all that comes from that person, poor, simple, disarmed, unmasked, defenceless, deprived of all those protections he had so elaborately prepared. Stripped. And yet nevertheless, he realizes at the same time that it is such a rush of wealth and life that there is certainly no greater wealth than this, no other life than this; to have a heart available, accessible, sensitive, exposed, uncovered, attentive, open, happy, live, alive, living — amongst all those who tremble with fear behind their armour.

To be sure, love weakens us. But this weakness is the ground, the only ground in which the strength of God can grow within our lives, that strength of God which is nothing else than what we call weakness. When God said that he loved, he had to translate this into terms of human weakness. God so loved the world...that he was weak enough to allow himself to be crucified by it! God died of his love for the world.

We like starting to love but it hurts to carry on. To love is a terrible thing. To love means to allow ourselves to be stripped, to lose all our autonomy, all our strength in order to please another. To love means to give ourselves away, to abandon ourselves. The Passion of Christ was that everything could be done to him. The Passion of Christ was the revelation of the terrible power we had over God because he loved us, because he gave himself to us, because he *is* love.

It is not possible to translate this into human terms without suffering. There is no better manifestation of God than his suffering. Once more, our religion is the religion of a crucified God; that is Revelation. His love is a love

47

equal to the greatest possible suffering: "No greater love is there than to give one's life . . ." Vulnerability, attachment, uprooting, tenderness, interest, anxiety, expectation, anguish — all these are nothing else but love. It all strips, it all causes suffering. Because once we enter that kingdom, we are for ever dependent, we must abandon for ever self-sufficiency, the security of self-sufficiency.

But you will object that God suffered only as a man. We should not understand it like this. God became man in order to reveal to us — to expose to us — what he was. For this purpose, to teach us divine values, he had to choose certain human values in preference to others. For all time he has chosen, elevated, consecrated some, and he has discarded the others. Those he has discarded are glory, wealth, power, honour. And he has chosen poverty, obedience, suffering, death. Love unto death. These are the human values that in God's view revealed his. These are the echoes in our dwellings that God has found to be the least unfaithful to him.

When God became incarnate, he did not, to make himself more attractive, take on human features that he did not possess: all that he took from our human lives — poverty, trust, humility, love, patience — were virtues which in some obscure, mysterious way were divine. God is familiar with this. God is at home with the poor, with those who love, with those who suffer; he knows what it is. He is at peace with those who love, who wait, who weep. He is familiar with the greatest suffering. All those who love, all those who are poor, all those who suffer find a fatherly, brotherly, warm, experienced welcome from God. A well-spring.

Jesus wanted to have the help of another man to bear his cross, a woman to wipe his face, companions to watch and pray with him, apostles to pass on his message, and then others to continue, so that his body, offered each morning as food, be eaten, so that his name be hallowed.

Lord, because of this power which you have given me, this responsibility which you have entrusted to us, since if I do not come the name shall not be hallowed, the kingdom shall not come, the will shall not be done, since a liturgical office has been allotted to me, an office to which you have personally called me by attracting me to you . . . here I am, I come. Lack of faith in the importance of the part we have to play is what prevents us most from praying. It is not the part of a dummy.

Most Christians are like those shareholders in limited liability companies who accept the idea of being ignored and do not claim their right — which is a real one — to manage the concern. From time to time they collect their dividends; and they sigh when things go badly. In the business of salvation, we accept the idea of not being of much account, of saying "Amen" from time to time (not often) of finding that things are going badly, that nothing can be done about it, that it's no use trying to understand . . .

"But you are a holy nation."[2] We have a royal priesthood to exercise. We are of God. "Of God" is a name. "Teresa of Jesus", Peter, Paul, James, John of God. We are all of that family. We all bear that name. We all belong to God.

Religion does not merely consist in believing that God loves humanity; it consists in believing that God loves me. And if the note which he expects from me is missing from the chorus of praise which he expects, then something is

[2] 1 Pet. 2:9.

missing to his happiness. Why have we such difficulty in believing what, nevertheless, we thirst after so much?

This is the deepest and most essential mystery of religion: "And we have recognized the love God has in our regard and made it our belief."[3] What makes our religion unique in the world, is that it asks us to believe that it is God who has loved us first. "You have not chosen me", said Jesus, "but I have chosen you."[4] Our own love is but a pale, careless, weak response compared to what he feels for each one of us. Do we believe him?

It is not just a question of believing that God loves humanity. This is very easy to admit and calls for no effort, for the very good reason that it doesn't mean anything. We must believe that this love is true, living, sincere, that it is therefore concrete and directed towards each one of us, down to the smallest detail. "But a hair of your head shall not perish",[5] not a single one of your illusions, not a single one of your acts of loyalty, not a single one of your enthusiasm, not one of your gestures of goodwill, not one of your impulses of trust and confidence, nothing of you will be degraded or lost without his being warned, touched, hurt. God really loves you. You interest him personally, passionately, continually. His joy comes from you, you are necessary to him, your heart delights him, he is dismayed by your indifference, tortured by your bitterness. He lives with you in a continual relationship of expectation, pride and sorrow.

If we do not believe this, if our life is not buoyed up by such an assurance, we have not yet begun to be Christians. On Judgment Day, the first thing we shall be asked is: "Did you believe that God loved you? Did you believe

---

[3] John 4:16.   [4] John 15:16.   [5] Luke 21:18.

that God waited for you, knew you, desired you, day after day?"

We all experience an invincible aversion to believing in it in this way. Yet it is only by believing in it in this way that we begin to understand the mystery. It does not make sense to believe that he loves "the others", if I do not believe that he loves me. It is only when I start from here that I will appreciate what an admirable thing it is that he should love the others. Otherwise I am, without realizing it, making out reasons for him to love the others ("who are good people perhaps"). When I can come to believe that he even loves me — that unsufferable creature whose burden I alone am able to judge — then I will realize the unfathomable depth of his unbelievable love.

The saints are those who will be able to say: "I have known the love that God had for me, and I have believed in it." We, on the other hand, would more likely have to say: "I was not able. I was often told, I often heard sermons on the subject, but I thought it was a manner of speech, a consolation, a charitable lie, a pious encouragement."

This is where the difference lies between a saint and ourselves. Yet no one better than a saint can measure his own inadequacy, the fearful inability of man to enter into the orbit of God, the fearful reluctance of man to renounce in company with God, the frantic sum of refusals which paralyse us all against him.

C. S. Lewis wrote: "Perhaps you have imagined that this humility in the saints is a pious illusion at which God smiles. That is a most dangerous error. It is theoretically dangerous, because it makes you identify a virtue (i.e. a perfection) with an illusion (i.e. an imperfection), which must be nonsense. It is practically dangerous because it

51

encourages a man to mistake his first insights into his own corruption for the first beginnings of a halo round his own silly head. No, depend upon it, when the saints say that they — even they — are vile, they are recording truth with scientific accuracy."[6]

Nevertheless, we must agree to co-operate in this invention, this will of God, which each one of us is. This is the first act of faith, of hope, charity which God asks of us, and it is the one which we usually deny to him until our dying breath.

It is only in the last pages of his diary, a few minutes before his death, that Bernanos's "Country Priest" manages to say: "I am reconciled with myself, with this wretched shell of mine. It is easier than we think to hate ourselves. Grace consists in forgetting ourselves. But if all pride is dead within us, the grace of all graces would be to love our own selves humbly, like any of the suffering members of Jesus Christ."

God loves . . . those to whom he can give most, those who expect most from him, those who are most at his mercy, those who bear the greatest burden, those who are the most committed, the most abandoned. It matters little to him whether they be pure like St. John or defiled like Mary Magdalen and Zacheus. What matters to him is that they should love and lean on him, rejoice in him, live only through him. God loves the humility, the open-mindedness, the candour of those who, being honest enough to know that they are not very lovable are nevertheless simple-minded enough to believe that they are loved and expect everything from him.

God loves those who, knowing that they are dull, are

[6] *The Problem of Pain,* London 1946, pp. 55-56.

yet convinced that they will do marvels — because God lifts mountains when, with faith, we ask him to do so. The spirit of poverty above all is this: that capacity to uproot, to disturb, that eager and constant ability to be roused (moved, set going) by the loving influence of God.

Coventry Patmore once said that the first impulse which gave a religious train to his thoughts was this idea which came to him accidentally, "What a wonderful thing it would be if there was a God with whom I could have relations of love and obedience". And with prodigious speed the feelings he evoked arose in his poetic imagination. He felt that he was lifted up to the nobility of the filial state which is a just balance between tenderness and respect, pride and modesty. How wonderful it was to play freely in his presence, how delightful to depend on the Father, to trust to his will, to rely on his love, to be able to reach him, touch him, honour him, to delight him by everything we invented for him. These sentiments came so easily, so eagerly, so naturally, that he could not help thinking that he would find truth by penetrating into this new world. He had never been happy like this before. And he set out to find the Father because for him there was no other truth than to be a son.

We do not believe that we are sons, we do not believe in the power we have over the Father. "The Father always grants my requests", that is a filial word.

Prayer is the only effectual act of which we are capable. Everything is decided, everything is prepared, everything is worked out, there in that active passivity. It is on these occasions, when we are silently and earnestly available, that God is able to prepare at that level of our being of which we are not aware, where everything which we will become

53

takes root and thrives, the seeds of what we shall appear to do and of what will actually be done by us.

But it is not possible for us to believe that God loves us without believing that that love gives something valuable. By insisting too much on the gift and on the gratuitousness, we lose the notion of the existence of the gift, of its contents.

Not only does the love of God make us do what we would not have done, it makes us become what we would not have become: a being infinitely more open, more docile, more yielding, more happy, more joyful, more refreshing than the one we would have forged ourselves, and whose distressing image we insist on keeping.

God alone knows what he expects of us, all the people he has made dependent on us, the gestures that he expects of us. When we despise ourselves, we despise all these plans, all these wishes of God that are within us, all that joy that God had expected of us, all that hope that God had placed in us.

> — Yes Lord, I know, your eyes saw me. But what am I in the crowd of this world? And have you looked at so many besides me.
>
> *Jesus.* — I saw you alone.
>
> — Then, no doubt, you saw me with a distant look, like a vision that vanishes amongst thousands of others. Tell me the moment when you had that thought for me.
>
> *Jesus.* — I have always had it.
>
> — Lord, tell me this too, during those hours, from what have you suffered most?
>
> *Jesus.* — From you.
>
> — Alas, Jesus. You bore the sins of all, their weight

was increasing but, tell me, with what thorn did I pierce your forehead?

Jesus. — With all of them.

— What, Lord, and it is I too who scourged you, and I too who nailed you, and I who killed you. Then, Lord, what did the others do?

Jesus. — You are my Passion.

— Then, my Saviour, your soul was distressed and afraid. Tell me, what did you fear most?

Jesus. — To lose you.

— Yes, Lord, I know that the lost should make your Passion useless. But tell me, are there many who get lost? Is it true that their number is greater than that of the elect?

Jesus. — If I lose you I lose all.

— But again Lord, what did you want, what did you desire most at that moment?

Jesus. — To save you.

— You were dying for all men and you thirsted to save them all. When you wanted all men so ardently, could one alone quench your thirst?

Jesus. — I thirst for you.

— Lord, how mysterious this is. How is it that I alone, if I am lost, make your Passion useless? And if I am saved, I take from you all regret for having suffered? And what share will the others bring to your victory?

Jesus. — Be my victory.[7]

Our catechism teachers used to discourage us when we were young by making a distinction between God's

[7] V. Poucel, *Évangile du pécheur,* pp. 76-77.

55

intrinsic glory which is immutable and inaccessible and his extrinsic glory which is dependent on us. But what is the use of extrinsic glory, what purpose is served by procuring it, if it has nothing to do with intrinsic glory? We appear to be surplus to requirements. This is precisely the distinction which should never have been made. We do matter to God, we have not been left out of his calculations, we have entered, we are introduced into the centre of the divine life. *"Filii Dei nominamur et sumus"*; that we should be called and should be the sons of God.[8]

"I fill up those things that are wanting of the sufferings of Christ in my flesh."[9] If something is wanting in the sufferings of Christ, then something is wanting in the honour of the Father? Then we have a purpose: to hallow his name.

What will heaven consist in? It will consist in saying the Our Father. There, we shall be able to say: Father, thy name *is* hallowed. For they alone will dwell in heaven, who are fully pleased, fully content to say this. For heaven is for those who are sufficiently interested in the business of the Father, who have lived enough on earth buoyed by that wish, for its realization to satisfy them.

The "business" of the Father is not that which provides security, calm, and prestige. That, quite rightly so, is not his business. Therefore, all those who do not love the poor, who dislike the sick, who hate suffering, who trample absent-mindedly on the humble, who consider humility to be dangerous and love abnormal — all those have rejected him. The manifestation of God starts by being the manifestation of our hearts. What has our own heart become attached to? Has it become attached to all those values he

8 1 John 3:1.   9 Col. 1:24.

56

has loved, taught, practised, or to prestige, power, our social dignity, our "legitimate ambitions", or to a serenity that knows no suffering?

Will we be happy in that heaven where the Our Father will be said? Do we dream of the day when we will be able to say: "Father . . . thy name is hallowed! We've done it. It has cost us dear, but now nothing is wanting in your joy and nothing is wanting in ours."

God would not be God; God would not be Father, if, when giving himself to us, he had not taught us to love and to give ourselves. The glory of God consists in having become God in everything. "Father, glorify thy Son, that thy Son may glorify thee",[10] said Jesus. That is to say: "Father, allow me to show how I dare love my Father, so that the whole world may know how you have taught me to love, how you know how to love."

God has placed his glory in lifting up all those poor, selfish, vague, wavering, sluggish little men. He wished to teach them, to inspire them with his love. The hallowing of the name is not our own personal holiness. It is the manifestation of the holiness of the Father breaking through ours. It is for this, it is for his greater glory that we give thanks to him at all times and in all places.

[10] John 17:1.

Thy Kingdom come

By means of his grace God enables us to accomplish actually that action which we try to exercise clumsily by means of natural prayer — stir up the inertia of God, improve his productivity, excite his mercy—that caricature of a religion, which we practise all too often. We can really do him good, hasten and assist the coming of his kingdom.

"Thy kingdom come!" When we say this, most of us think — if we think at all — "as late as possible". Are we waiting for the end of the world? Impatiently? Have we prayed this morning "that this world may pass . . ."? The early Christians never ceased saying: "Marana tha — May our Lord come."

Do we look forward to the day when we will drink all together in the kingdom? "And I say to you, I will not drink from henceforth of this fruit of the vine until that day when I shall drink it with you new in the kingdom of my Father."[1] God is waiting for us. Are we anxious to meet him again? "The day of the Lord shall come . . . in which the heavens shall pass away with great violence, and the elements shall be melted with heat and the earth and the works which are in it shall be burnt up."[2]

[1] Matt. 26:29.   [2] 2 Pet. 3:10.

Every time we say the Our Father with sincerity, we hasten the advent of the kingdom. Do we not, though, try to ruin it all? At the very moment when we say "Thy kingdom come", do we not deep down in our hearts pray that it should not come? That nothing should be dissolved and that this corner of the world, where we are so snugly settled, should not "pass away"? Do we realize that in this way we delay, each one of us, the kingdom and the joy of the Lord.

We should not think that importance attributed to man, to the prayers of men, to this influence of men one over the other, is contrary to the sense of the transcendence of God. "You know not where it will please God to unwind his ladder," said Ruskin. This is fine. And it is true. But he willed roads, meeting-places. He has asked us to help save the world. A Christianity which rejects all intermediary between God and man is no longer Christianity.

If God only gives his grace vertically to individuals who cannot communicate anything of this grace to each other, if God never gives me anything which can transform me for ever, if he has never given me anything that I can pass on to others, then he has never given me anything. If God has not given me something that I can give, he has never given me anything of himself, for he is gift.

But God loves us so much that he wants us to love too. He wants to be God in everybody. He is not proud to be the only one to love. He is proud of making others love, of spreading his love, of propagating himself with us, through us. It is easier to act than to make others act. The masterpiece of God's love is to have won man to this movement.

We only know God insofar as we have allowed him to

59

work within us. We only know forgiveness when we have learnt to forgive. We only know the love we have received when we have given ours in exchange. To others. That is what brotherhood means. God has willed this "horizontally". God has willed that we should be indispensable one to another; that is what is meant by the Catholic Church.

"For it became him for whom are all things and by whom are all things, who had brought many children into glory, to perfect the author of their salvation, by his passion . . . that he might become a merciful and faithful high priest before God."[3] "So Christ also did not glorify himself that he might be made a high priest, but he that said unto him '. . . Thou art a priest for ever, according to the order of Melchisedech'."[4] According to the order of Melchisedech, according to the order of a religion founded before him. He has inserted himself in a pre-established, a pre-existing order. In this line — a horizontal one — which began centuries before (with Melchisedech) and which continues through the Church, now and for ever.

This means a terrible thing: that God has bound himself to us. That there will be men who will not be saved because others have not prayed *pro totius mundi salute,* as the Church asks us to do every morning at the Offertory. ("We offer thee, Lord, the chalice . . . for our own and the whole world's salvation, Amen.") He could, of course, have done everything on his own. But he wanted us to have some share in the work. He asked for it. "He that believeth in me, the works that I do, he also shall do: and greater than these shall he do."[5]

Then, will some be damned because of the inactivity of

[3] Heb. 2:10-17.   [4] Heb. 5:5-6.   [5] John 14:12.

60

others? This, we object, is a scandal. No! It is a mystery. God has trusted us to such an extraordinary extent that he believes that each generation will provide him with souls, with hearts that are free and considerate, obedient and loving. That there will always be men who will agree to say: "Our Father", that he will obtain this from us.

God believes that love will prevail: "Have confidence... I have overcome the world."[6] Every time we suffer, fail, miss, yet continue to love, we prove—we make true again— that word of the Lord, that trust of the Lord. We confirm it. The world *is* overcome; I love still! Thy kingdom come!

Let us recall the words of Claudel: "Not one of our brothers, even if he wished, could let us down, and within the most cold-hearted miser, the prostitute or the vilest drunkard, there lives an immortal soul that breathes in a holy fashion, and which, deprived of light, practises adoration in the dark. I hear them speak when I speak and weep when I kneel. I accept everything! I take them all, I understand them all, there is not one that I do not need, that I can do without. There are many stars in the sky and their number exceeds my power of counting, and yet there is not a single one that I do not need to enable me to praise God. There are many above, but we hardly notice a few that twinkle, whilst the others stir within the chaos and within the vortex of a dark vase; there are many souls, but there is not a single one with whom I do not commune through that sacred place within it which says: Pater noster."[7]

We must accept the idea of finding reflections of God

---

[6] John 16:33.
[7] *Cantique de Palmyre. Conversations dans le Loir-et-Cher.*

in poor fellows who are like us, just as others — strange though it may seem — find some in us. "Oh, miracle of our empty hands," wrote Bernanos "marvels of God's grace, that are more beautiful in men's souls than in our hands that have been the mediators."

St. Paul had long ago written: "For God who commanded the light to shine out of darkness, hath shined in our hearts to give the light of the knowledge of the glory of God in the face of Christ Jesus. But we have this treasure in earthen vessels, that the excellency may be of the power of God and not of us. In all things we suffer tribulations but are not distressed. We are straitened, but are not destitute . . . But having the same spirit of faith, as it is written, 'I believed for which cause I have spoken', we also believe. For which cause we speak also . . . For all things are for your sakes; that the grace abounding through many may abound in thanksgiving unto the glory of God."[8] Paul had "a sting of my flesh."[9] It is believed that they were epileptic fits. It couldn't have been very pleasant for a preacher. Thrice he asked the Lord to release him from it. It would certainly have increased his output, his efficiency, his influence. Surely the Lord ought to have realized the severe handicap which this sting was likely to place on the apostolic work of such an essential nature that was being entrusted to him? But the Lord replied: "My grace is sufficient for thee."[10]

Treasures in clay vessels; this is the dramatic reality of the Catholic Church. "He hath done great things in the humility of his handmaid".[11] And we must continually accept the — scandalous — mystery that the infinite com-

---

[8] 2 Cor. 4:6-15.   [9] 2 Cor. 12:7.   [10] 2 Cor. 12:9.
[11] Luke 1:49, 48.

municates through the finite and that perfection is received through imperfection. That God entrusted himself for ever to our earthly hands.

The tragedy of the Church's condition consists in the lack of proportion between what we are and what we give. We have received from another all that is good in us. Christ warned us of this when he said: "And call none your father upon earth: for one is your father who is in heaven. Neither be ye called masters, for one is your master, Christ."[12] "Blessed is he that shall not be scandalized in me."[13] Jesus has said this. And it concerns us all. The salvation of some depends on us all, on the loving prayer of each one of us. The first Christians prayed, and their prayer was a living thing because they loved. And they loved so well because they prayed. (It is always the same path: we become sons by becoming brothers and we become brothers because we become sons.)

When Christ gave us the Our Father, when he asked us to say it in his name, when he decided to give us rights on the heavenly achievements, he associated us for ever with his work. We must believe this mystery; henceforth there is something of God in us. All our missionary spirituality rests on this belief; we have only received in order to give.

God so loved the world that he sent his Son, his sons, his daughters into the world. To save the world. Like himself. Through him, with him, in him... "The Son of God suffered unto the death not so that men might suffer", wrote George Macdonald, "but that their sufferings might be like his."

"... Jesus should die for the nation. And not only for

[12] Matt. 23:9-10.   [13] Matt. 11:6.

the nation, but to gather together in one the children of God, that were dispersed."[14] We too are in the world for this gathering. The children of God are everywhere, but they know it not. They must recognize one another and gather together through us. We must give them the opportunity of knowing to what spirit, to what Holy Spirit they belong. This is the witness that God expects from us.

"And when all things shall be subdued unto him, then the Son also himself shall be subject unto him that put all things under him, that God may be all in all."[15] The perfect beatitude of Christ will not begin until he hands over to the Father, the whole world conquered by him. Christ is Jesus and every one of us. He is the Head, we are the Body. It is not over; the desire of Jesus is there, it is waiting for ever.

"With desire I have desired to eat this pasch with you, before I suffer."[16] If he desired with such a great desire to eat that pasch with us before he died, do you not believe that he will desire with an even greater desire to eat with us that pasch of perfect rejoicing? "For I say to you that from this time I will not eat it, till it be fulfilled in the kingdom of God."[17]

Don't you think that the Lord, who knew the happy brotherhood of friends gathered round the same table, yearns with a mixture of sadness and hope, to find it again? "And I say to you, I will not drink from henceforth of this fruit of the vine, until the day when I shall drink it *with you* new in the kingdom of my Father."[18] This happiness of the Lord depends on us. Why are we

[14] John 11:51-52.   [15] 1 Cor. 15:28.   [16] Luke 22:15.
[17] Luke 22:16.   [18] Matt. 26:29.

64

not more anxious to join him? To go and share with him that wine which he refuses to touch until we are all gathered round him?

The elect are also waiting. St. Thomas says that "the resurrection of the body will not add a negligible quantity to those souls that are redeemed". In some ways, hope still exists in heaven. What they are hoping for is that reunion of the children of God, scattered all over the earth, which has been entrusted to us, and their hope is now directed towards us. We must go and join them, we must bring the others, as many of them as possible. As soon as possible. By saying, in the most filial manner possible: "Our Father . . ."

"And this Gospel of the kingdom shall be preached in the whole world, for a testimony to all nations; and then shall the consummation come."[19] The day the whole world knows, has understood that the hour has come to "pass" from this world to the Father, it will be the end; we shall pass. And it will be the perfect pasch. Shall we not try to spread the tidings, the glad tidings a little better? "Jesus Christ will not be whole until the number of saints is complete," said Bossuet.

What a task we have been given! Are we proud of it? And are we heart-broken because things are not going better? Do we find there is a painful contradiction between what could be done — by us to God — and what we do? Do we groan with exhaustion, shame, and impatience over the birth of the redemption? Is this the drama that causes us our deepest humiliation, our most harassing revolts, our most unbearable sufferings? For those who know that they are harnessed to this yoke the weight is

[19] Matt. 24:14.

so heavy, appearances are so discouraging, the path some-times so bewildering that they can only carry on by stopping from time to time to remind themselves to whom they belong, what they are doing, why they are doing it.

When men trapped in a mine by a fall of rock try to dig themselves out, and have burrowed for hours into the walls without being conscious of making any progress, they begin to wonder in the end whether their efforts are not useless, whether they serve any purpose at all . . . There comes a moment when they stop, exhausted. Then they lift their heads silently, they prick up their ears and far away in the distance they hear other knocks, faint and distant but constant and regular, which slowly wearing down the same resistance, are laboriously moving to-wards them. Then they find courage to start work again in spite of fatigue and of the dark. Every time they are exhausted, they stop for a second to listen again — and to believe.

We too must stop knocking — during the hours of prayer, in our retreats, at set times when we pause for breath during our life — to hear once more what has called us to this task, to allow the faint echo of that other world towards which we are going, to reach us; that kingdom of the Father where we are expected, in order to remind ourselves that we have faith and in whom. "Have confidence, I have overcome the world"; "God has so loved the world . . ."; "God was in Christ, reconciling himself to the world"; "When I have risen from the earth, I will draw all to me."

Risen from the earth means, on the cross. The Church will never be a success here below. The only way for the Christian is exodus. It is a painful way. The Church will continue to be in the desert until the Second Coming. (If we feel that we are in the desert, it is because we are in the Church.) It is for ever regretting the comforts of Egypt, the "flesh pots of Egypt", the comforting results, success, palpable efficacy, moderate conquests, authority, prestige; "When will we govern — When will you restore Israel?"; when will we be able to settle at last?

"For a mixt multitude of people, that came up with them burned with desire, sitting and weeping (the children of Israel also being joined with them) and said: Who shall give us flesh to eat? We remember the fish we ate in Egypt free cost. The cucumbers come into our mind, and the melons, and the leeks and the onions and the garlic. Our soul is dry: our eyes behold nothing else but manna."[20]

Nothing else! Nothing else but manna! Nothing else every day but the gift of God. And tirelessly God pushes us on every day a little further. Along the path of sorrow, of crucifixion, of painful expansion.

Outside the Church there is no salvation. But what happens within? Just think of our neglect of our responsibilities, our fearful lack of seriousness, our indifference to what is happening in this world where God is thirsting for men, . . . our passivity. Are we on the way? Or rather are we still busy nibbling at the onions and cucumbers? Dreaming of them anyway.

When I have risen from the earth . . . . In spite of his apparent failure, we must believe in the efficiency of God. And we must believe in ours too, in spite of our poverty. Like Martha and Mary at the time of the death of Lazarus, we are always tempted to say, "Lord, if thou hadst been

[20] Num. 11:4-6.

here, our brother had not died,"[21] things would not have gone so badly, we would not be so dead . . . And we forget that things never go so badly as when he is there. Where the Cross is, he is there; where injustice is, he is there. To be a Christian consists precisely in believing that through all this bitterness, he saves the world.

We have to serve a Mass which is infinitely beyond our grasp. The server is indispensable. Someone must answer, must correspond. Without us there would be no Eucharist. We are responsible. We must carry on without giving way to despair. Perhaps on the last day we shall find that a few faithful souls, a few fiery souls were sufficient to make that evil which so overwhelmed us, caused us so much anguish, worry, and torment, also serve for the coming of the kingdom.

Until the last saint has said the last Our Father, all can yet be saved. If we prayed enough, it is still possible that no one would yet be lost, because from the beginning of time, God has foreseen our prayer.

Léon Bloy wrote in *Le Désespéré:* "Every man who performs a free act, projects his personality into infinity. If grudgingly he gives a penny to a poor man, that penny will pierce the hand of the poor man, will fall, will perforate the earth, will bore through the suns, will cross the firmament and endanger the universe. Should he commit an impure act, he will perhaps darken the heart of thousands whom he does not know but who correspond mysteriously with him and need this man to be pure, just as a traveller dying of thirst needs the glass of water of which it is spoken in the gospel. An act of charity, a gesture of real pity will sing for him the divine praises

[21] John 11:21, 32.

68

from the days of Adam till the end of the world; it will cure the sick, console those in despair, calm the storms, ransom prisoners, convert the infidels, and protect the human race."

There is no past, no future, no yesterday, no today, no tomorrow. There is but one Christ in every one of us, who is, who was, and who will come, and who says: "Our Father".

Thy Will be done

THE REDEMPTION is not ready-made; it is in the making. It is not complete; it is at work and requires our collaboration.

In order to make it genuine and valid, our whole life must be the extension, the image and the fulfilment of our prayer, and on that account there is nothing more effective than to pray, in proportion to our faith. It is only if we have asked for a long time beforehand that his will be done, that we will have the strength to do the will of God and help see that it is done everywhere.

Obviously our spontaneous and natural prayer will be: "My will be done." It is true to say that our ideal is to become more and more independent, self-confident, authoritative, autonomous, self-sufficient . . . or to become more and more considerate, submissive, docile, obedient. Obedient unto death. Like God! Like our God, not like the God that Adam thought he was imitating; our God, whose will is to do the will of another — "not what I will, but what thou wilt" — whose joy it is to place his joy in another — "Here is my beloved Son in whom I am well pleased."

God terrifies man; he is total self-denial. He is entirely

directed towards another, like a bird that is nothing but flight. He knows no rest, no satisfaction, no withdrawal within himself. He is perfect ecstasy towards another. We, on the contrary, have a personal subsistence which leads us always to rely upon ourselves. We want to be both ourselves and love at the same time; that is the mistake.

Man is a being that does not dare to complete himself. He loves, but he fears sacrifice. He loves to give, but he is terrified of losing. When children play, they give and then take back again. We must, however, choose between two pleasures: to give *or* to possess. When we give ourselves . . . we are no longer our own masters!

Man is always frightened as soon as he realizes that he loses himself by giving himself. It is a terrible feeling, a leap in the dark. And we are afraid like that child on the roof of a house on fire. Below, his father calls on him to jump, saying that he is there and that he will catch him in his arms. But the child sees only the smoke that blinds him, and a terrible feeling of anguish prevents him from obeying. Nevertheless we are asked to believe that the Father's arms await us beyond that black hole into which we must leap in order to live. And begin again every day on the basis of this dizzy trust, this absolute surrender.

We are always trying to do our own will whilst doing the will of God, to transform ourselves whilst remaining as we are, to become transfigured without losing our appearance. We are always tempted to escape from God and to become independent. It is too painful a thing to be dependent, it is too painful a thing to love; we want to be free.

Freedom, however, does not consist essentially in being able to choose. True autonomy is the power to be

71

able to determine for ourselves, to dispose entirely of ourselves, so as to give ourselves to others. And refusal, the fear of giving, is an inability to be available and therefore an absence of true freedom. If "the ego exists only to be laid aside" — he who wishes to save his life shall lose it —, to keep it is the worst failure of all. It is only when we give up what we held to so desperately that we will receive it; the day when we entrust ourselves to the Father.

Christ delivered himself up. He did in the midst of suffering and humiliation what Adam had failed to do in the midst of peace and joy: "Into thy hands I commend my spirit." We must learn to allow ourselves to be fashioned by God over a long period of time: "Be it done to me"—for a long time, patiently. We must accept his rhythm. Simon of Cyrene, who was ordered against his will to climb to Calvary carrying the Cross of Jesus, was unable to carry it up there all alone at his own pace — the pace of a healthy man. He had to drag it along at the same pace as the exhausted victim, he had to learn to fall in step with another's step, he had to accept another's rhythm. And little by little, under the burden of the cross, he ended by becoming mindful of that silent companion who preceded him. At first he only saw the cross, but he ended by seeing only Jesus. This is what is asked of us too.

If we allow ourselves to become embittered and discouraged by the sight of evil in the world, our indignation will merely increase the evil. We will only be able to bear it without aggravating it with the weight of our anger if we walk beneath the cross at the same pace as Jesus.

Is there anything more tormenting, more unacceptable than the redemption of the world? It seems shocking that

72

there are only 500 million Catholics knowing the truth. Why? Why not the others? Why didn't that neighbour of mine, so much more generous than I, receive the same revelation? Why does God allow so many good people to go astray, so many hypocrites to steal his message, so many impostors to distort its propagation, so many rich men to defraud the poor of it, so many liars to mislead so many simple souls, and so many that are satiated cause so many starving men to loathe the real food, the real justice, the real truth of God?

Despite all appearances, despite everything, we have to believe that "God enlighteneth every man that cometh into this world",[1] that there are enough saints in the world, that there is enough holiness within the Church to lift up the whole world. But in the meantime . . . what about those who die without ever having met that God whom perhaps they would have served, loved and pleased so much more than we do? Beyond our shock however, we must believe. We must believe that the plan that God has chosen to save the world is better than anything that we could imagine; that the redemption of the world is a mysterious thing and that it is taking place in spite of all appearances. We must not tolerate injustice, yet tolerate that God should tolerate it.

This is what was asked of the priest-workers: a heart-rending acceptance, a faith that went beyond scandal, in spite of scandal, giving up what appeared to us to be the most urgent, the most obviously just and necessary form of atonement. This was the only thing that God could still demand from those beloved sons who had given up everything else to follow him, the only thing which he

[1] John 1:9.

could still give them to give, the only deeper fulfilment of their devotion.

"So Christ...who in the days of his flesh, with strong cry and tears, offering up prayers and supplication to him that was able to save him from death, was heard for his reverence. And whereas he was the Son of God, he learned obedience by the things which he suffered."[2]

We all know that a Christian must bear the cross. In theory we are all prepared to accept one. But you will no doubt have noticed that the cross that comes our way is never the right one. The cross we bear (our health, our face, our straitened circumstances, our family, our stupid job, our failure — or our stupid success) always seem to us to be intolerable, mean, humiliating, harmful. It is precisely the one that should never have come our way, the one we cannot possibly accept for all kinds of obvious reasons which we never tire of repeating. Every other one would have been better, our neighbour's; the previous one, the one we should have thought of. Ours is hateful, it destroys us, just think of it, it hurts us. It embitters us and therefore gives us the right to have a grudge against everyone! Desperately we call for another, a cross made to our own size, a cross which will be bearable, spiritual, elevating, beneficial to ourselves and to others.

But if the cross suited us, it would no longer be a cross, and if we refuse those that hurt us, we will refuse all crosses. The cross which God sends us must of necessity always be humiliating, painful, paralysing, difficult. The cross is precisely what hurts us in that place where we are most disarmed and vulnerable.

The cross is what is unbearable. The will of God is

---

[2] Heb. 5:7-8.

74

exactly what is unbearable to us. God is unbearable, impossible to live with, intolerable: "Can you drink the chalice that I shall drink?"[3] It took Christ a whole night of agony to say "Thy will be done". Jesus himself took a night, a whole night of sweat and blood, to accept the fulfilment of God. He too suddenly found his cross intolerable, impossible to live with, unbearable. And "with great cries and tears" he asked to be released from it.

What separates our will from that of God is not so much the fact that we are sinners, but that we are men. And our will as men ceaselessly urges us to reject the offer made to us to become God. For with our bodily eyes we see as crucifixion, passion, and death, those things that make the happiness of God—mutual gift, abnegation, preference of Another.

"When he was crucified, he did that in the wild weather of his outlying provinces, which he had done at home in glory and gladness."[4] From all eternity the Son makes restitution. Eucharist. From all eternity, he gives himself, he entrusts himself to his Father and there is no greater act of joy than that. For the space of an hour during the solemn procession of centuries, heaven opened a little and in a flash we witnessed the eternal happiness of God: it was Calvary. "None can see God and live" says Scripture.

Mary, who had imagined a very different kind of life, a very different kind of holiness, was the first to accept to die to all her plans. Mary was the first to accept that the redemption should take place in the way we do not want it to take place: ruining all our plans, all our expectations,

---

[3] Matt. 20: 22.
[4] G. Macdonald; Cf. C. S. Lewis, *The Problem of Pain*, p. 140.

causing them to fail: "Be it done to me according to thy word."[5]

Mary agreed that God should deprive her entirely of all those things that Adam would have claimed — to control the situation, know where one is going, know where one is, see the whole position clearly. Mary is the one who, without any of the privileges of Adam (immortality, impassiveness etc.) placed her trust in God. Without question. Ignorant, suffering, condemned to die. Mary allowed herself to be led in a way totally different from what she had expected, in a quite different way from what she had imagined, not knowing where she was going.

Mary said to God: "Be it done to me according to thy word";[6] thy will be done, and God fulfilled her wish too on account of her holiness. She learned what it would cost. It began at once. At once she was humiliated, upset, annoyed. She had renounced maternity and she had to take on one which was so extraordinary that it transformed her whole life. Her betrothed quarrelled with her. Think of the humiliations, the sadness, the loneliness, the problems that were strewn across her path. From a distance, it all seems simple to us. We must take the trouble to imagine the avalanche of events, and Mary, very young, loving and desolate, facing them.

Like every one of us, it is because of his demands that Mary recognized God. God alone could hurt so much. God alone could torture thus. God alone could insist on coming in such a painful and difficult way into a life destined, to all appearances, to become just as trivial and sterile again.

God alone could bring about such scandalous things.

[5] Luke 1:38.   [6] *Ibid*.

After the Annunciation, the misunderstanding with Joseph, the birth in a stable, there was the massacre of the Innocents. "And his mercy is from generation unto generation...He has exalted the humble...He hath received Israel his servant";[7] so many babies of Israel massacred, so many families of Israel plunged into mourning! And she had to accept all this and see no contradiction in it. And she had to continue singing "*Magnificat*". She had to continue believing that God was good, that God wanted all this and that these were the "great things" that had to be done. That it all looked a failure, but that it was only apparently so. That it was in this way that he was going to save the world.

Afterwards, it was worse still. Afterwards, nothing happened at all. Afterwards, for thirty years, it looked as if in the end nothing would ever happen at all.

Then, when, at last, something did happen, Mary was again pushed around, baffled. "Woman, what is that to me and to thee?"[8] One day Jesus was told: "Thy mother and thy brethren stand without, desiring to see thee." She listened. Where is the mother who would not listen to the answer of her son, her boy who in spite of everything has not forgotten her, who is going to show everyone how he still loves, how he still respects his mother? Yes indeed! "My mother and my brethren are they who hear the word of God and do it."[9]

Some of the words spoken to Mary in the gospel seem to us to be very harsh. But Mary was always ready to hear them. It was thus that she knew, that she was faithful. She knew perfectly, she felt perfectly, in this way she was in the greatest possible communion with her Son and was

[7] Luke 1:50, 52, 54.　　[8] John 2:4.　　[9] Luke 8:20-21.

preparing for the total communion which he was to ask from her. It was thus that she was preparing for the day for which she had been created from all eternity, for the day when she would say that "Be it done", of which the first, the early "Be it done" of the Annunciation, was but the first joyous answer of a child. There, on Calvary, she will say no longer only "Behold the handmaid of the Lord" — that was still easy — but "Behold the servant of the Lord — be it done to him, be it done to us . . ." It is there that Mary became fully mother, it is there that she gave all, it is there that she met all the thoughts, all the wishes, the whole mission of that man who was both her Son and her God. There, she bore him a second time: in his redemption, in his work. Because she gave her perfect consent.

On Calvary, Mary became by the same gesture, fully mother and fully daughter. She had learned "though she was but a girl, how to obey..." He had taught her. By making demands on her which none of us could have endured—to such an extent that we attempt to disguise them behind all sorts of interpretations—he had detached her and lifted her up to him: "When you have lifted the Son of man" and the mother of the Son of man. On that same mountain of suffering, he had shaped her to the greatest possible likeness of himself. She was liberated of everything which he took from her. And, behind her suffering, she blessed this nearness, this resemblance, this increasing agreement, this identification with him, which was the cause of all her suffering, of all the suffering he caused her.

Without understanding, she clung to everything. With complete trust. Every day she had to start again to recognize God in her life in a different way from what she had expected. And day after day she continued to believe that through the poverty, the disappointment, the overwhelming, the suffering, the torture of the handmaid, the Lord was doing marvels.

God disappoints us. Since the Incarnation, God has never spoken the language we expected of him. Jesus disappointed everyone: his fellow countrymen, his apostles, his forerunner . . . and now, each one of us.

"From that time, Jesus began to shew to his disciples that he must go to Jerusalem and suffer many things from the ancients and scribes and chief priests: and be put to death and the third day rise again. And Peter taking him began to rebuke him, saying; Lord, be it far from thee, this shall not be unto thee."[10] And St. John the Baptist from his prison cell, sent a messenger to find out whether really there was nothing better to look forward to: "Art thou he that art to come, or look we for another?"[11]

They expected a triumphant, thundering God who would be manifest and would dispense justice. Now God had decided to reveal what was not known of him, what was most intimate, most personal, most tender in him — his love. He manifested himself to us by those long hours on the cross.

We walk among his enemies, who said to him: "Come down! Show yourself to be God! Give us an argument, a sign that will silence them, some unanswerable success which we can show to all these heathens who do not think like us—a Church of which we can be proud!"

But Jesus has not come down. ("You know not of what spirit you are."[12]) He continues to suffer. He is for ever revealing the infinite patience of divine love. And for ever we try not to understand.

He would not come down from his cross and manifest

[10] Matt. 16:21-22.   [11] Matt. 11:3.   [12] Luke 9:55.

his power, even if the whole Church, gathered together in an enormous congress, were to beg him to do so. But he comes whenever a humble priest in some wretched hut pronounces the words of Consecration. Because he loves to be defenceless, offered, hidden, at our mercy, abandoned to our negligence, our rudeness, our impatience, our whims, our contempt. That is his language. There is no longer any other. Will we reject him because we ourselves would not have made him like that?

Many of us are really waiting for Antichrist: someone who will succeed, who will do something, who will make all men brothers within the same authority, instead of waiting, like God, for all men to agree to be brothers within the same love. We will all be brothers the day we all know how to say: Thy will be done. And the more we say it, the more we will learn how to say it.

We must believe in the efficacy of our prayer. We should also use it as a means of consulting God, and await with confidence to be enlightened by it. If we pray long enough, the time will always come when we will cease thinking about what we are asking for, in order to think above all about him from whom we are asking it.

"As I hear, so I judge."[13] To hear, we must listen. For a long time. "The Son cannot do anything of himself, but what he seeth the Father doing."[14] To see, we must look. Prayer means looking, contemplating. And when we contemplate, we become after a time similar to what we have been contemplating. To contemplate means to change. It means starting to look like him whom we look at and to mirror the Face we address. To change us is the greatest possible fulfilment of our prayer.

[13] John 5:30.   [14] John 5:19.

Prayer is a transfiguration. To be thus transfigured is the greatest possible miracle that we can obtain. "But we all, beholding the glory of the Lord with open face, are transformed into the same image from glory to glory, as by the Spirit of the Lord."[15] We are transformed . . . if we allow God time to act. He alone can perform that miracle which is far more startling, far more difficult, than to change water into wine.

"Thy will be done"; let us allow God time to make these words ring truly in our heart.

Our prayers are hypocritical because we want them to be perfect. "Oh my God, I firmly believe . . ." Come off it! At the very slightest disappointment, we are desperate. "I wash my hands in innocence . . ." Really? Let us say a truthful prayer: "I do believe Lord: help my unbelief,"[16] said to our Lord the father of the child who was possessed. He was honest; he knew himself. Let us beware of sublime prayers and of all the lies they make us tell.

Jesus himself suffered anguish. "Now is my soul troubled. And what shall I say? Father save me from this hour. But for this cause, I came unto this hour. Father, glorify thy name."[17] He needed a whole night of agony to overcome his disgust. "Father, let this chalice pass from me . . . Nevertheless not as I will but as thou wilt."[18]

Let us not try to pretend that we are capable of accepting everything at once. We must share the weakness of the Lord before sharing his strength. Let us moan, let us protest, let us complain in all sincerity, rather than pretend to accept at once something which is beyond our possibilities.

Let us beware of perfectionism. By that I mean a very

[15] 2 Cor. 3:18.   [16] Mark 9:23.   [17] John 12:27-28.   [18] Matt. 26:39.

serious spiritual illness, the first symptom of which is a hasty, vain, or presumptious spontaneity to do that good which we know must be done, without placing ourselves or allowing ourselves to be placed in the state of mind which will enable us to do it. When we say "Thy will be done", do we not usually think: "It must be done all the same, so let it be done! Let it be done at once Lord, and let us hear no more about it."

Resignation never comes from God. Jesus was never resigned. "But that the world may know that I love the Father . . . Arise, let us go hence."[19] It was with enthusiastic consent that he went forward to his Passion: "Father, the hour is come; glorify thy Son that thy Son may glorify thee."[20]

So long as these words are not on our lips, we should not go forward towards a sacrifice which is not meant for us. Because our hour has not come. There is nothing more dangerous than to anticipate God's intentions, nothing more pharisaical than to wish to be worthy of God before we have understood that he loves us when we are unworthy. Before we have acknowledged, before we have rejoiced over the fact that he loves us when we are unworthy. There is nothing more opposed to the spirit of our religion than to want to be the father of God, to be the one who takes the initiative of giving.

God gives, even the joy (the real joy, not a heroic make-believe smile) of sacrifice, sacrifice seen in its real light; a greater identification with him. Sacrifice is a stimulating choice. We should not make it, so long as we only see in it a "renunciation". It is not sadness but joy that God expects

[19] John 14:31.
[20] John 17:1.

from us. (". . . that they may have my joy filled in them-selves".[21]) To give up the world is to prefer God.

"So that the world should know that I love my Father let us go from here." We must *love* the place where he will take us, where we will find him, and we must prefer it to the place we are about to leave. On no account must we not want to go there. But we must not move so long as we dislike the idea. So long as we are in that state, all that we are to do is to hope that in spite of everything, God will change us, God will rejoice us not elsewhere but in this very place that chills us with fear. God is strong enough, powerful enough to perform the miracle; that we should be happy bearing that unbearable cross; that this uprooting should make us feel rich, satiated.

God does not want to take away our luggage — it is of no interest to him — but our attachment to our luggage. What he asks us to do is not to give it up with the energy of despair, but not to be attached to it any longer.

Many Christians, driven by pious zeal, race along the platform to jump onto the train of perfection. As their luggage gets in their way and slows them down, they throw it away with a sublime gesture, and climb into their carriage. But as they proceed on the journey, the satisfaction of not having missed the train decreases and they begin to think increasingly about the luggage. One item, then another. Such a good instrument! Such a comfort for the apostolate! All the things I could have done if . . .

They realize that they are disabled, resentful, envious. Because of their haste, they have abandoned everything before they knew what would have liberated them, what would have taken the place of everything. There is only

[21] John 17:13.

one intelligent thing to do. Pull the emergency cord, get down, take a taxi, and retrieve this luggage which obviously we still need, which we cannot yet do without.

And once our bad temper due to this travel incident is over, let us begin once more to hope, with humility and simplicity, that God will distract us, that he will absorb our attention sufficiently to enable us to forget one by one all these accessories of our sanctification.

God alone, after long prayer, can change us to the extent that we are willing to accept what, in the first place, we rejected with all our energy. Provided we allow ourselves to be guided by him. We must be really schooled by the precepts of the Saviour, formed, transformed by his Spirit of love, to be able to say the Our Father, truly to make bold to say: "Our Father!"

To learn how to pray, there is but one secret: for a long time say very short prayers. Say: "Father". Then stop when we see that we do not think it. Start again. Then as we don't succeed, pray that we should succeed. Say: "Thy will be done." Wait long enough to measure the extent to which we do not want it, the extent to which this idea repels us, terrifies us, makes us want to escape. We should stand still however and repeat it, a little better now; thy will be done. We should allow the pain caused by this attempt to be sincere and break away, to die down. And then we should pray again, so as to come to think it absolutely, desire it absolutely: that thy will be done.

Give us this Day our daily Bread

IF WE separate this request from the impulse which carried those that precede it, we debase its meaning. This is the time when the faithful usually come into action; it is a distressing habit. They are silent so long as it is a question of God's honour, his kingdom, his will. But they rush in to ask for their bread. It gives this part of the Our Father a fearfully selfish look. Whereas if we look at it within the same (supernatural) perspective as the others, it is the most despoiling of all requests.

Who is it amongst us who is expecting his daily bread from God? Every day? (Give us *this* day.) Without caring for the morrow? We have made the most careful plans to ensure tomorrow's bread. And that of the day after tomorrow. We will work as long as it is necessary. Because we can only rely on ourselves! If we had to start relying on God! Yes, we are willing to say so for form's sake because it seems to please him. But he must not be afraid that we will take him at his word . . . If he wants to add a little cake . . . we will think it nice of him. But as far as serious things are concerned, we really can't begin to dream.

Were we to mean it when we say: give us this day our daily bread, we would at once be accepting poverty, which

85

consists in expecting everything from God alone. The day we come to rely on God alone for our daily bread, we will have the soul of a poor man. We will no longer be like the son who asked for his birthright so as to go far away and settle his business on his own.

Give us today...means agreeing to come and ask for it again tomorrow. It signifies trust. It means accepting, rejoicing over the fact that our life depends entirely on him. It means agreeing to be not self-sufficient, neither materially nor spiritually, even for a second. God wants us to be pilgrims, living from day to day, without ever settling anywhere.

When we base our day on the effort of the day before, we already cease to be a traveller. To be a Christian means to accept being perpetually uprooted. Every morning we must begin our day again as we might begin our life again, without knowing what purpose it serves, without understanding, beginning each day again by not understanding any longer, by expecting again everything from him. To ask day after day for our daily bread, means accepting cheerfully to limit our care and our anxiety to the interval between two communions. In the desert, only a day's supply of manna could be picked up. The rest rotted.

Wealth corrupts itself and corrupts us. We never realize it better than when we are deprived of it, and we experience that curious impression both of disaster and of simplification. Nothing makes us understand the beatitudes better than that strange sensation of relief which we experience in times of catastrophe.

A trivial little earthquake, and suddenly, the earth shuddered under our feet . . . We felt terrified, yet at the same time mysteriously unburdened. We were back to scale. We were reminded that we mattered little, that we could do nothing on our own ... In a flash we were freed from that exhausting illusion which consists in believing that we must ourselves secrete our life. When catastrophes happen, we suddenly understand that our life does not depend on us, that we have but to receive it, that everything is given to us, second by second, and that we must do nothing but expose ourselves, that we must do nothing but surrender ourselves. We are out of breath as we carry the stolen burden of our independence. And it is the exhaustion produced by this harmful pursuit which causes us to be so tense, so congealed, so disagreeable, so rigid, so hard.

After a bombing raid, we all spoke to each other in the street! Every passer-by we met was a wounded brother. What the bombs destroyed most were the walls round men's hearts. We witnessed — and what a fine sight it was! — men speaking to one another. But for that to happen, it was necessary that they should become poor. When the war was over, we pretended once more not to know each other. Once more we were submerged in our different callings.

When we have little, we give all. As soon as we have more, we give less. Our satisfaction consists in what we have, but we are anxious not to lose anything, to continue to be "satisfied", to conserve this beginning of security, of safety. "Woe to the rich", because wealth enables us to do without — or at least makes us believe we can do without—God. It enables us to do without love, it removes us from union with God, it ex-communicates us from God and from our brothers.

But if wealth enables us to do without God, the knowledge that we have a Father enables us to do without wealth. Those who tear themselves away from the pleasure of enjoying his gifts in order to look at him who gives, to give him thanks, and lift their eyes towards the face of the Father, discover such a look of tenderness that they are freed for ever from anxiety and worry.

All the teaching of Jesus is aimed at making us learn to prefer God. Not to "renounce the world" but to prefer God. And know that we profit by the exchange. And therefore to be happy. Those who trust are happy. Do we trust God? If we do not trust God, we should no longer call him Father!

We bristle with suspicion. Every day we blaspheme against the goodness of the Father: "It was too good to last"; "It is always like that" etc. We criticize everything that is sent by God. We fear all that he has in store for us. What do we expect from God? At the slightest alarm we fear the worst, like nervous children in a car, screaming at every corner and wanting to snatch the wheel from the driver's hand, instead of saying to ourselves: "All is well, it is the Father who is driving. I am not afraid."

If we have really said, if we have thought: "Father", all is well. We are cured, overruled, we have surrendered. But our only concern is to protect ourselves against him, against the "unexpected": this is the name we have given to Providence. To provide too well for our children is to shield them from Providence. Is this really the way to love them, to do them good? We are, of course, the representatives of Providence as far as they are concerned. Of course we must act, but contrary to what we might think, our action is paralysed, crushed, by the constant discouragement of people who do not know that they have a Father. It is correct to say that what the Father gives us above all is the means to work, our hands before our bread. Chesterton once remarked that we thank the infant Jesus once a year because we have found sweets in our stockings, and that we would do far better to thank him every morning for finding a good pair of legs in them. But our real wealth is to know that if we were to lose everything, our bread, our hands, our legs, we would still have a Father. That is the wealth which, above all, we must pass on to our children.

Instead of doing nothing any longer, we shall have the strength to lift mountains, if we know that it is the Father who sends us there, that he needed someone . . . to cheer up that man, that woman, those children, to sanctify that work, to accomplish that task, to love all those beings that surround us. And we will then do it with that steadfastness of people who have been entrusted by another with a responsibility that they have not chosen. The great problem is to achieve that balance, enough prayer and enough work, enough improvidence and enough foresight, to avoid being disheartened or carried away, and thus being distracted from the essential.

We must have an immense respect for our work, because it comes to us from the Father: and we must perform it with complete optimism, because we are in his hands and he has promised to take care of us, whatever happens.

We must avoid praying like this: Lord save me because we are perishing. We are hungry, feed me. It really is a question of *our* bread. Perhaps then what we are asking for is the courage to give to our neighbour his daily bread. If we are the "temple of the Holy Ghost",[1] if we live now, not we, but Christ liveth in us,[2] if God is in us, perhaps it is with our hands, with our money, with our friendship, that he has decided to be "providence" to this one or that of our brothers.

Thus by repeating every day "Give us our bread"

[1] 1 Cor. 6:19.　　[2] Cf. Gal. 2:20.

whilst we have perhaps more than we need in our cupboard, we are maybe asking him to change our hearts of stone into hearts of flesh . . . a miracle far greater than to multiply bread and fish.

Poverty is not in itself a virtue. But love is a virtue. Therefore the virtue of poverty is to love our brothers enough and to trust God enough to allow ourselves to become impoverished for their benefit.

"Father, all that is thine is mine": we have seen that it is much more than a gesture of gratitude or the result of reflection which leads us to add: "And all that is mine is thine"; it is an identification. Therefore, since "what is thine" is to give . . . I too must give what I allow thee to give through me.

Poverty is a theological virtue. So is humility, because, like poverty, it is but another name for love. God is poor. God came into the world like a poor man. He gave up all which would have interested, attracted, or impressed us: money, power. He chose a state of poverty, not in order to conceal himself, but to reveal to us what he loved, what he was.

God is poor. He has nothing with which to reward those who love him. He is love. He knows only how to love. All that he can give us is to teach us to love as he does. Which one of us could bear the terrible poverty, the terrible destitution of God? He keeps nothing for himself. He lives on gifts just as it is also said of the poor that they "live on gifts, they live on charity". Those who love him must know it and be stimulated by his love, "strengthened by his strength, rejoiced by his joy, because he has nothing to give them".

In the divine family one owns only what one gives. Have we not experienced this too? We own only what we give, and the only real happiness is that which we have been able to give to another.

Jacques Rivière, in the diary which he kept as a prisoner of war, describes the happiness which he experienced when, having shared out the contents of a parcel he had received, he suddenly became poorer than all those amongst whom his property had been shared. We know where this joy comes from: by becoming poorer, we become more of a son, by giving all we become like the Father.

Either we place all our joy in giving—and we will be happy in heaven, "rejoiced by his joy", the only kind that can reign there; or we will understand nothing about this joy which is "against nature", "paradoxical" — and heaven will mean nothing to us. When we come across these people who love each other — and spend their time doing so — who keep nothing for themselves, who share everything, who "sacrifice" themselves and look as if they find it fun and appear to enjoy the game, we will feel completely out of our element.

"Rejoice with his joy . . ." We must not analyse poverty studiously. But if within a short while charity does not give us the experience of a taste of heaven, does not soon make us prodigal and poor — those two divine vices which a reasonably-minded Christian does not forgive — it is a good thing from time to time, to test by one of our actions whether we really place our trust in the Father and our joy in the joy of others.

Spiritual writers have discovered a very comforting word: "To offer our goods means nothing. We must offer ourselves." Many have found this to be the heroic solution. With one bound they scale the peak of sanctity. But their wallets remain intact. As far as we are concerned, let us take out a note from time to time "to see whether it hurts". Let us learn that words alone are not enough.

"When I get up, I offer my day to God," said C. S. Lewis, "but I have hardly shaved before I have taken everything back." We must be careful not to spend our lives being satisfied with formulas. A good Christian once said to me: "I never go to High Mass; it makes me waste the whole morning." He had certainly "offered his whole life" more than once to God. My whole life, but not my Sunday morning!

We have to choose between two kingdoms, that of God or of the riches of this world, that of God or that of human success. The kingdom of God or that of prestige, connexions, influence and of all forms of wealth, material and otherwise. Our only wealth, our only security should come from the knowledge that we have a Father.

Jesus in his stable was far richer than any one of us. Because he had a Father and he knew it. He who has a Father finds that this is enough. To become poor is to learn to be content with God. Blessed are the poor: theirs is the kingdom of God. We make bold to say "Our Father". This is a possessive case; what candid boldness! We do what we like with a Father. But do we really believe it? Are we really bold enough to say: Our Father?

"Lord, shew us the Father, and it is enough for us", said Philip.[3] If only we could say that sincerely! We have been shown the Father. We will really be sons when, day after day, he suffices us.

Often, it is when asking for bread that we think of those for whom we had promised to pray. It is strange to think that, through intercession, we can in a way influence

[3] John 14:8.

God, and make him look on someone more favourably than he would have done of his own accord. Jesus has become incarnate to such an extent that it is in us that he has allowed himself the possibility of praying for men. Through men, by men, he gives himself to other men. God has given us a real supernatural efficacy over others. God has willed that salvation should be a communal adventure. God is a "father of a family", a large family.

Prayer gives us supernatural power over others. When a saint prays for us, he really has an effect directly on us. To love one another "in God" does not mean loving one another from a distance. We are in God, and our love will not have a long journey to make. To love one another in God is to love in others what there is of God in them. And let God, in us, love the others. The more we belong to God, the better we will love. Our sense of solitude, said Emmanuel Mounier, is our awareness of all the things within us which we have not yet made spiritual.

The flesh isolates. It is the spirit that communicates. A medieval author wrote: "When you are at prayer you are in my presence and I am in yours. Do not be surprised because I say 'presence'; for if you love me, and if it is because I am the image of God that you love me, I am as much in your presence as you are in your own . . . and I, in my turn loving God, love you. So seeking the same thing, tending towards the same thing, we are ever in one another's presence, in God in whom we love each other."[4]

Those who have outstripped the materialism of a request that is too selfish, end up by saying: "Then, the daily bread is the Eucharist?" No. It is all bread. The

---

[4] Cf. De Lubac, *Catholicism,* London 1950, pp. 31-32.

"Our Father" was instituted before the Eucharist. The daily bread of the "Our Father" is everything that must feed our soul and our body, because life does not separate one from the other. Sometimes it will be a bitter bread, but always a nourishing bread.

Every time that Christ bowed, he was fed and strengthened. "And what shall I say? Father save me from this hour. But for this cause I came unto this hour. Father, glorify thy name. A voice therefore *came from heaven:* I have both glorified it and will glorify it again."[5] In Gethsemani, "there appeared to him an angel from heaven, strengthening him".[6]

Is God harsh? Yes, sometimes. He is a father, not a doddering old grandpa. He respects us sufficiently to believe us worthy — capable — of suffering. "For it became him for whom are all things and by whom are all things, who had brought many children into glory, *to perfect* the author of their salvation, *by his Passion.*"[7]

Let us not say: "God has taken this, that . . . from me. He deprives me." No. When we suffer a privation, he means that he has given us as much as he knew how to give: to make us give in turn. If God calls us to sacrifice, let us not force, let us not cut ourselves the bonds that hurt us so much. Let us offer ourselves to God. Let us allow God to become God in us. Let us remain silently before him, until by dint of gift and love he lifts us enough to enable us to give and to love in turn.

When we suffer, the Father follows us with his eyes, with the same solicitude, the same admiration, the same anxious tenderness, the same wish to rescue and to help as when he looked on the Son as he went towards his cross.

[5] John 12:27-28. [6] Luke 22:43. [7] Heb. 2:10.

Forgive us our Trespasses

Do WE really want him to? When we make this request, are we not as hypocritical as when we say "Our Father" without wanting to share anything, "Thy kingdom come" whilst thinking mainly of ours, "Thy will be done" whilst endeavouring to impose ours on him? Do you often go to confession? How long is it since you last confessed? A month? three months? a year? And you pretend that you wish to be forgiven?

To be forgiven by someone we have offended does not just mean seeing that life with him continues as if nothing had happened. The solution we most readily adopt with those we brush against is to appear "not to take any notice". And this applies to God as well! That is why we go to confession as infrequently as possible. His implicit forgiveness, which we are promised under certain conditions which we have carefully studied, is sufficient for us.

Have we therefore never known the joy of admitting our guilt, of saying so, of going to see the person we have offended ("I will go to my father and say to him . . ."), of going to see him open his arms like the Father of the prodigal son — "And when he was yet a great way off his father saw him and was moved . . . and running to him . . ." — and of going to see his joy burst forth on finding us again — "And they began to be merry."[1]

As this feast takes place every time we come back, why don't we come back more often? Why are we such misers with God and why do we so rarely give him the joy of pressing us to his heart? We do not like "explicit" forgiveness, yet God is never more God than when he forgives.

God is love. He is gift. It is he who gives grace. But the strongest love is the one that overcomes the main obstacle, ingratitude: the perfect gift, the perfection of giving is to for-give, and the greatest of graces is to pardon. If we were not sinners, needing forgiveness even more than bread, we would not know the depth of God's heart.

"There shall be joy in heaven upon one sinner that doth penance, more than upon ninety-nine just who need not penance."[2] How is it that a sacrament which causes so much joy in heaven, inspires so much repulsion on earth? Pride as usual, the wish to cut ourselves off, to be self-sufficient, to isolate ourselves. What in the end do you prefer: to be a sinner and that God should forgive you, or be without sin but without the revelation of the love of God? To be pleased with yourself or to be pleased with God?

Absolute humility will alone enable us to bear cheerfully the comparison between our indignity and the splendour of God. C. S. Lewis has written: "It may be that salvation

[1] Luke 15:11-32.
[2] Luke 15:7.

96

consists not in the cancelling of these eternal moments (of sin) but in the perfected humility that bears the shame for ever, rejoicing in the occasion which is furnished to God's compassion and glad that it should be common knowledge to the universe."[3]

Nothing is more dangerous for our spiritual life than to wish to become "worthy" of God's love for us. We will never know God better than when we have got to know the extent of our sin. It is through the immense, tireless patience of his forgiveness that we measure the immensity of his love. We must be careful lest our repentance becomes merely a wish to be in order. "Quits and free." We go to confession to be "quits". Quits with what? Quits with whom?

Instead of enabling us to think no more about God — about the gift, the unbearable forgiveness of God — because we no longer think of our sins, confession makes us enter a new life in which it is no longer possible to think of anything but him. God tells us: "Shut up! Stop talking all that nonsense! Do you believe in me? Do you believe that I love you enough, that I care enough for you, that I have enough affection for you, that I rejoice enough at the slightest gesture you make in my favour to forgive you even this stupid confession, which is one more sin?" If we know that we are forgiven, loved in this way, we will be so overwhelmed with joy and gratitude that we will no longer be tempted to sin! That is the meaning of absolution.

Perfect contrition, imperfect contrition? Requisite conditions? We complicate things to such an extent that we forget *the* condition without which all confessions would

[3] C. S. Lewis, *The Problem of Pain,* p. 49.

be farcical: to believe that God loves us. "We have known and we have believed the charity." And, "In this is charity: not as though we loved God, but because he hath first loved us."[4]

To go to confession is to go nearer and love and be loved by God. To go again and hear that God loves us. To begin to believe in it. And to discover at the same time that we had never understood that it is of this that we had to ask forgiveness, and not of that litany of ineptitudes which only serve to mask our real destitution, our real refusal.

In *All Glorious Within*[5] Bruce Marshall describes the confession of an old sailor dying in a hovel. At the end, when the priest asks him: "Are you sorry for all this?", the dying man who was sincere could not help saying "No". These were the only pleasant memories he had, these were the only occasions when a little happiness had come into his life. "These girls were the only people ever to be nice to me." And the priest, impressed by the truth of this admission, which was so much more accurate than what he usually heard, just said, "Can't you at least be sorry that you are unable to be sorry?" Can't you be sorry that you have not believed in a love which surpasses to such an extent these feeble joys, that had you known it, it would have satisfied you; you would not have searched elsewhere, you would not have done all those silly things to stave off your hunger. That kind of sorrow is infinitely more moving than all our vague regrets. We always make that mistake. We deplore actions so as to take our mind off the real cause, which we do not want to give up.

When there is a corpse in a pond, bubbles rise to the

[4] 1 John 4:16, 10.   [5] Published in U.S.A. under the title: *The World, the Flesh, and Father Smith.*

surface nauseating and alarming. The mortified owners of the pond then do everything they can to suppress the bubbles and ensure that the surface is clear again. They even call in experts to make sure that it doesn't happen again. But if the expert says: "Sir, it's quite useless to clear up these bubbles, others will follow; you must take your courage in both hands, dive in and find the corpse"; that, never! But "You are paid to clear up the bubbles. Clear them up and then leave us alone."

This is exactly the attitude of most penitents. "Father — I don't know how this could have happened to me . . . a boy brought up as I was, a leading member of Catholic Action like me, well . . . well, I have made a bubble. Father, this is terrible, please clear up this bubble." On the other side of the curtain, the confessor takes a deep breath and asks: "My son, do you pray?" Somewhat taken aback by this diversion, the penitent then usually supplies information of no use whatsoever. "I forget my morning prayers, but I nearly always say my evening prayers." The priest takes another breath and then resumes: "My son, do you live habitually in the presence of God?" This time, the penitent in his corner becomes restless and impatient. "Oh blow!" he says to himself "This is just my luck, I have fallen on a mystic!" He has one wish, one desire, one need, that his bubble should be cleared up, and as far as everything else is concerned, he wants to be left in peace. He wants to be told to "go in peace"; that is what he has come for. Thoroughly annoyed, he ends up by saying "Father, I am very busy. I have a lot to do: work, family, children, charities, I have no leisure. Yes, I think of God . . . when I have time."

What can we answer him, except that it is no use

clearing up this bubble, that he will make others. To live in the world without sinning is like walking on the waters without sinking. It is a miracle. Who can be saved? To this question, "Jesus looking on them, saith: With men it is impossible, but not with God. For all things are possible with God."[6]When St. Peter held the hand of our Lord tightly in his, he walked on the waters as he would down the street. But it is purely through the mercy of God if those who want to walk alone, who want to walk by themselves, notice by getting wet, that they are sinking.

It is lucky for a sinner that there are bubbles, that there is something to point out to him the serious nature of his condition. Our sins are alarm signals. Yet we go to confession to get the signal system cut off! We must hope to be cured every time. Every time we must hope to get the corpse out. But to do this, we must agree beforehand that it is there.

As we enter the confessional, we say: "Bless me, Father, because I have sinned", because I have received this first, this great grace of realizing that I have sinned. We do not say: "Punish me, Father, tell me off because I have sinned." But we say: "Father, say a good word to me, encourage me, congratulate me, because God has touched me: I have realized that I am a sinner."

Those who faced Jesus felt that they were sinners. They discovered that they were sinners. We would not have confessed to Jesus as we confess ourselves now! That kind of formality we go through to restore our looks, to restore our countenance . . . It would have cost us dearly. We would have known at once what we were lacking,

---

[6] Mark 10:27; Matt. 19:26; Luke 18:27.

what was our greatest fault, the one we had never admitted and which explained everything else. Under his gaze, we would at once have seen ourselves as we are. His love would have made ours spring from the depth of our barrenness, from the depth of our sterility. We would have seen what we had become by beginning to rediscover what we ought to have been, what we ought to have become.

Those who met Jesus, witnessed the awakening of immense unknown parts of their being, which until then had always been compressed and bruised. They could no longer recognize themselves because, from the depth of their being, they felt the surge of infinite impulses of joy, tenderness, generosity, gratitude, because they had discovered that the Lord knew them, that he had searched for them, waited for them from all time. The Lord had called them by their name.

The story of Zacheus[7] is that of each one of us. He had climbed a tree to see who Jesus was. And he heard himself called by his name: "Zacheus, make haste and come down." Jesus calls him by his name! Jesus invites himself into his home like an old friend! He speaks to him in a familiar way. He jokes with him, "Make haste — come down!" Now, as the gospel says, Zacheus was short and rich; quite probably he was also fat. He couldn't have been used to climbing trees. Experienced climbers know that it is easy to climb up — but to come down is another matter. "Make haste and come down" said the Lord. That confession began with a laugh! Zacheus toppled down with surprise. His confusion and joy were such that he had lost control of his senses. Jesus trusted

[7] Luke 19:1-10.

him. Jesus loved him. It was in his, Zacheus' house that Jesus had chosen to come. His head was in a whirl: he had lost his sense of reckoning. He began to give half his goods to the poor, and if he had wronged anyone, he restored him fourfold. What was he going to have left? He couldn't care less. How had he ever been able to care for all that! Henceforth, he had another treasure: God loved him.

"Behold I give." Now he too felt generous, good, just, happy. He would for ever remember that extraordinary moment when he passed from his satisfaction with his money to his satisfaction with God.

When we reach heaven, Zacheus will tell us what a skinflint he was and how good God is to have forgiven him all that at one go, and how powerful God is to have been able to change him thus, and to have succeeded in getting him, Zacheus . . . to give!

"As we forgive those who trespass against us" is not a bargain. It does not mean: "Lord, see how I forgive, therefore forgive me yourself . . ." We must understand it to mean: "Forgive, and we will forgive like that, we will know how to forgive like that." There is indeed one thing which proves that we have not received forgiveness, it is that we do not know how to give it back. There is one thing which proves that we have not received the love of God, it is that we do not know how to give. "Behold I give" said Zacheus. For we only know how to give what we have received.

The basis of the doctrine is sound. Who was the first to forgive? Who was the first to love, to give? The Father without doubt. There can be no possible hesitation. It is not you who have forgiven and God who has imitated your forgiveness. It is God who has redeemed the world, who has so loved the world, that he has given his Son in order to forgive the world.

Like the people of the Old Testament, like the brother of the prodigal son, they grumbled, these "good" people under whose very nose Zacheus led Jesus into the house he had acquired by doubtful means. "If all you need do is to be a profiteer, to be honoured by his visit, I can't see why one should be scrupulous. It's always the sharp types who get the best of it! We now know what we must do to be appreciated!" (That's exactly what you would have said, wouldn't you?) Everyone blamed God for being too good.

Jonas, who was sent by God to help convert the Ninivites, found nothing more consoling, more illuminating, more encouraging to say to them than: "Yet forty days, and Ninive shall be destroyed!" Yet forty days and Ninive shall be destroyed! And the people of Ninive repented all the same. "And the men of Ninive believed in God: and they proclaimed a fast and put on sackcloth, from the greatest to the least . . . and God had mercy with regard to the evil which he had said that he would do to them, and he did it not." And what about Jonas? Jonas was furious. He wanted to die. He no longer wanted a life where things happened. "I beseech thee, O Lord, is not this what I said, when I was yet in my own country? Therefore I went before to flee into Tharsis, for I know that thou art a gracious and merciful God, patient and of much compassion and easy to forgive evil. And now, O Lord, I beseech thee take my life from me: for it is better for me to die than to live." Then God was "too good" to him as well and instead of punishing him for his hardness of heart, he invents the whole adventure of the ivy, so full of humour, kindness, and affection. "And the sun beat

103

upon the head of Jonas . . . and he said (again!): 'It is better for me to die than to live.' And the Lord said to Jonas: 'Dost thou think thou hast reason to be angry, for the ivy?' And he said: 'I am angry with reason even unto death'." Then, starting from his ivy and his bad temper, God explains to him. God apologizes. God pleads in favour of his mercy: "And shall not I spare Ninive, that great city, in which there are more than one hundred and twenty thousand persons?"[8] Tell me, Jonas! They do not know how to distinguish between their right hand and their left. Aren't you going to join with me in taking a little interest in them, join me in pitying them a little, loving them a little, forgiving them a little as I forgive you? With me, give them a little of what you receive from me at every moment of the day.

"Son, but it was fit . . .," explained the Father to the embittered brother of the prodigal son. These words echo the disappointment of God who continues to believe that we will share his joy, delight in his kindness, participate in his generosity and his mercy, associate ourselves with him, raise ourselves to the level of this feast.

The prodigal son left his father's roof because he had lost the faith. He no longer believed in the love of the Father. He wanted his share of inheritance to start business on his own. When he decided to return and ask for forgiveness, his heart was still dead, he believed he was no longer loved — he felt he was no longer a son. He came back to avoid dying of hunger. (This is imperfect contrition.) But the Father had been waiting for him for a long time; for a very long time he had rejoiced at the very idea that his son might return. Therefore as soon as he

[8] Jonas 3 and 4.

caught sight of him, he went out, he ran to meet him, he kissed him, he left him no time to finish his confession. He called upon his servants to dress him, feed him, and care for him.

Because so much love was shown to him, the son began at that moment of experience to be overwhelmed by that love. Remorse that he had never suspected overcame him. There in his Father's arms he began at last to measure his ingratitude, his cruelty, his insolence, his injustice. It is only then that he came back for good, that he became once more an open, trusting son. And a living one too: "My son was dead and is come to life again."

The elder son, the "just man", experienced a similar transformation. His case was far more difficult. We should not say that God loves sinners more than just men (if there are any just men!). A mother does not love her sick child, who gives her so much to do, more than the fit children who go out to play on their own. But she shows it in a different way. When it is said that the prostitutes will precede us into the kingdom of Heaven, we will not be left in the rear in so far as we are "just men" (this might encourage competition of a deplorable nature). It is in so far as we are people who refuse to recognize their sin, in so far as we are proud sinners, to whom God prefers humble sinners. More often than not we are whited sepulchres. Well painted-over, well camouflaged, well varnished, well arranged to keep up appearances. This is the imposture which God will not tolerate.

The elder son was perhaps in a state of grace, but there was certainly no grace in his actions. He had done nothing seriously wrong. "I have never transgressed thy commandments", but he had no love. His sense of justice had embittered him: "Behold for so many years do I serve thee and yet thou hast never given me a kid to make merry with my friends." — It was hardly worth while not going on the spree like everyone else! (He now begins to have a grudge against everybody because he has been so virtuous.) When one comes to think of the advantages! I never received any encouragement, and when he had spent every single penny, all that that little fool had to do was to come and weep great tears of repentance — simply because he was hungry — for the whole house to be turned upside down. And I am expected to behave like a mug and sing my part in this farce. Not on your life! They will eat their fatted calf without me!

The Last Judgement imagined by Anouilh comes to mind. The elect are waiting outside the gates of Paradise, vaunting their merits, and sure of their booked seats inside. Suddenly an incredible rumour spreads around. "It appears that he is forgiving the others as well!" This causes universal astonishment and indignation. They protest, they bewail their efforts and their self-denial, they burst out with imprecations against God . . . and at that very moment they are damned.

God has manifested himself, God has revealed himself as he who forgives, and they did not recognize him. Yet, were they there themselves for any other reason except that they had been forgiven?

We are prejudiced against the elder son, the embittered just man, and we are tempted to treat him far more roughly than his brother. We expect the Father to rate him for his hard-heartedness, punish him, and drive him out. But the Father was so good that he knew how to remove the venom, even from that heart. He was kind and patient with that son too. "His Father therefore coming out began to entreat him." The Father said most gentle and affectionate words to him: "Son, thou art always with me, and all I have is thine." And he apologized. "But it was fit . . ."

I feel sure that the heart of the elder son melted when he met with such kindness. He expected, he hoped for blame so that he in turn could blame, harshness so that he could be hard, anger to support and strengthen his own anger. But this humble and unexpected love disarmed him, and he too began to love like the Father, because he had found a love that he did not expect. He saw how the Father loved, and he could not help communing with and sharing this love.

"God alone knows how to remit sins." God alone knows how to make that gesture of grace, of gladness, of superabundance, that free gesture. It is difficult to make. The way we grant our forgiveness is often deplorable. In many families the members are no longer on speaking terms after they have forgiven one another. The look of superiority on the faces of those who forgive is so exasperating that the forgiven will never forgive them!

Much love is needed if we are to forgive well. The only forgiveness which we can give well is that which we have received from God. Once more, it is when we have understood the Father well that we become brothers. He to whom nothing is forgiven, does not love. He to whom a little is forgiven, loves a little. But he to whom a great deal is forgiven, loves much.

When we leave the confessional we should feel like throwing ourselves at everyone's neck. And ask for their forgiveness. "Listen! I was so silly that I thought I had something to forgive you. Now, I no longer know. Please be good enough to accept my forgiveness. I have received so much that I must share it. So take a share of this forgiveness with which I am overflowing. Forgive me for offering it to you so badly."

With one single gesture we re-enter into the love of God and the love of our brothers, into the communion of God and the communion of the Church, from which we had excommunicated ourselves through sin, through the state of sin. All forgive us when God forgives us. All love us when God loves us, but we also love them all when God has taught us to love again. (If this were not so, it would indicate that something has gone wrong and that we must go back again to confession.)

We love them all, we forgive all . . . However, let us be careful lest we forget someone. Someone exists who has disappointed and offended us, someone with whom we are continually displeased and with whom we are more spiteful than we would dare be with anyone else. That is ourselves. We are so often fed up with ourselves. We are sick of our own mediocrity, revolted by our own inconsistency, bored by our own monotony. We live in a state of indifference and even of unbelievable hatred towards the nearest neighbour that God has given us to guide and to offer to him. We would never dare judge any other of God's creatures with the contemptuous negligence with which we crush ourselves. It is said that we must love our neighbours as ourselves. We must therefore also love ourselves in the way we try to love our neighbour.

Therefore, we must ask God to teach us to forgive ourselves, to appease our wounded pride and our disappointed ambition. Let us ask him to allow the kindness, the love, the indulgence, the incredible trust with which he forgives us, to win us over to such an extent that we shall be freed from that dislike of ourselves which follows us everywhere, and of which we are not even ashamed. It is impossible for us to know God's love for us unless we alter our own opinion and feelings about ourselves, and side with him, even against ourselves, when he loves us. God's forgiveness reconciles us with him, with ourselves, with the whole world.

And lead us not into Temptation, but deliver us from Evil

THE ENGLISH translation "And lead us not into temptation" is really blasphemous. As if God could wish to "lead" us to do evil! We must never forget that the Aramaic language has not many shades of meaning. We cannot ask for the suppression of temptation, that is impossible. But we can ask: "Do not let us give way . . ." God tempts no one, says St. James. "Let no man when he is tempted say that he is tempted by God. For God is not a tempter of evils and he tempteth no man. But every man is tempted by his own concupiscence . . . Do not err, therefore, my dearest brethren. Every best gift and every perfect gift is from above, coming down from the Father of lights, with whom there is no change nor shadow of alteration. For of his own will hath he begotten us by the word of truth, that we might be some beginning of his creature."[1] God does not lead into temptation. God loves.

But he does us the honour of not preserving us from everything, like those mother-hens who bring up their children in cotton wool. God does not want the world

[1] Jas. 1:13-18.

to be like those bad schools where to make sure that all the pupils behave, they are always flanked by two masters and all the "occasions of sin" are timorously suppressed, so that at the same time, all occasions of consciously choosing not to sin are also suppressed.

Because we come "from below", everything is a temptation to us, and to demand the suppression of temptation would be to ask for the destruction of the world. Everything urges us to turn away from God, to seek for ourselves, to possess, to close our hands. But at the same time, everything is an opportunity to enable us to show our preference for God, to surrender ourselves, to open ourselves, to dispossess ourselves, to place ourselves in his hands.

We are thoroughly incapable of suppressing temptations, but we are free either to blame them on God — which means yielding to them — or to love him all the more on their account. "Unhappy man that I am, who shall deliver me from the body of this death?" cried St. Paul. But correcting himself at once, he added: "The grace of God, by Jesus Christ Our Lord".[2] There lies our liberty, which is the measure of our possibilities for love.

Great humility will alone enable us to make use of temptations as a means of access to God, as a means of intensifying our intimacy with him. Perhaps Peter would never have denied his Master if instead of saying: "Although all shall be scandalized in thee I will never be scandalized",[3] he had said: "Lord, it is going to be terrible. I will never manage it, come to my help, don't leave me a second." (The favourite prayer of St. Philip Neri was "Lord, don't trust Philip".)

[2] Rom. 7:24-25.   [3] Matt. 26:33.

We will falter at the very first hurdle. That is quite certain. We know it only too well . . . considering for how long we have begun all over again every day! We must ask the Lord to help us whilst thanking him for giving us continually this opportunity to measure his love.

But deliver us from evil: it is no accident that "evil" is in the singular. Evils will always be with us, and all the other parts of the "Our Father" have shown us how inevitable, useful, beneficial, "sacrificial" it is that we should have some. But we know well that there is but one evil, and that is sin.

And there is but one sin: not to love. To separate ourselves, to withdraw ourselves, to give up our possibilities of communication. Voluntary ex-communication, ex-fraternization, that is the sin. That is the evil which for ever tempts us and from which we must for ever ask to be delivered. Every time we commit that sin we have a foretaste of hell, because hell is nothing else but the final settlement of that state of refusal. *Libera nos a malo:* deliver us from "the evil". We are perpetually torn between two kingdoms, which we learn to experience, to know a bit better every day. For God wants us to choose our eternal fate with full knowledge of what we are doing.

Hell is not a place but a state. In actual fact heaven and hell have already begun for us. They are present in our soul, and they will never be present except there. We must dismiss from our minds the childish and ludicrous imagery of the mythological hells of Virgil and Dante. They are so terrifying that they end by tranquilizing us. Because when we say — rightly — that God is good, we dismiss almost automatically the idea that he might throw someone into boiling oil and the problem vanishes.

112

What is terrifying is the hell which exists in each one of us, that mania for destruction which is always smouldering deep down in our hearts, that latent despair, always ready to swamp everything, demolish everything.

"Love is strong as death, jealousy hard as hell", says the Canticle.[4] Love is as hard as hell. Hell, the taste of hell, the taste of annihilation has the same fury, the same fierceness as love. We fling ourselves into it with the same passion; we want to be sure that we have trampled down the last shoots of hope to such an extent that no longer will anything come to trouble that stillness from which we expect peace. "It hurts less to be dead than alive." And we decide not to move until death comes, to love no longer — to devote ourselves, perhaps, but not to expect anything in return, to expect no longer anything from anyone (in that way we will suffer no more disappointments), above all, not to believe that someone loves us (it hurts too much when we discover we were mistaken). In future we will try to manage alone, suffer alone, die alone.

For us, suffering is the deprivation of a good thing, and hell is so painful because it is the deprivation of a supremely good thing for which we were made: God who is love. God will never force us to love him. God leaves us free. If we want to go to heaven, we must choose to go there. If we are to be happy in heaven, we must love to love. (Metempsychosis is a solution that merely puts back the problem: it is not the number of attempts that will ever oblige us to say "yes".) God has done as much as he could. He has become incarnate. He has shown us a way. He has given his life. There is no greater love than to give one's life . . . What more can we ask him for?

---

[4] Cant. 8:6.

All things considered, says C. S. Lewis, the reply to all those who dislike the doctrine of hell, is itself a question: "What do you want God to do?" Wipe out all their past faults and at all cost give these creatures a new chance, smoothing all difficulties and offering every miraculous aid? But he did this on Calvary. Should he forgive them? They do not want to be forgiven. Leave them alone? Alas, I believe that is what he does. There are those who say: "Thy will be done." And there are those to whom God ends up by saying: "Thy will be done."

Just as heaven will consist in being able to say: "Father, thy name is hallowed! Father, thy kingdom has come, thy will is done", hell is in a way the Our Father upside down: "My name is hallowed, my kingdom has come, I enjoy alone and for all time the horrible liberty claimed by me to need no one, to depend on no one. My will is done."

Each one of us will go where our love is to be found: those for whom it is wealth will be for ever sated with wealth, those for whom it is the flesh will be sated with flesh, those for whom it consists in pleasing others will for ever commune with the joy of others, those for whom it is God will commune with the joy of God. Those for whom it is brotherhood, will be received into the eternal brotherhood, the brotherhood of the children finally reunited with the Son, the Brotherhood of Heaven.

We know the taste of heaven, the taste of renunciation, humility, trust, of communion with others, brotherhood, giving, forgiving, sharing. On the other hand, when we are unbearable even to ourselves, when we are discontented, vindictive, full of bitterness, resentment, when we are incapable of love or pity, we experience something of hell.

114

It is not God who damns. Men damn themselves. It is they who cut themselves adrift. Maurice Zundel compares these souls to houses drenched by the sun, but that close their shutters to the light so as to remain in the dark. Even in hell, light shines in the dark. It is darkness that does not want to grasp it. Even in eternity, God will not restrict man's liberty, but if he does not oblige anyone to love him, he never rejects either anyone who loves him or who wants him. One single gesture of love, one single sign of repentance, one single call for pity or forgiveness, and hell would end immediately. Then, many will say, "I'm all right. I'll never be as bad as that." Nobody is crazy enough to want to be unhappy, no one willingly wants to lock out God.

It is that you do not know what perversity exists in each one of us. Camus wrote: "When I was young, I lived with the idea that I was innocent, that is to say with no idea at all. Now . . . I know that I had the plague . . . I learned that, indirectly, I had assented to the death of thousands of men . . . This did not appear to worry the others or at least they never willingly spoke about it. As for me, I was aghast. I was with them, and yet I was alone . . . I continued to be ashamed, I learned that we all had the plague, and I lost my peace of mind. I am still searching for it today, trying to understand them all and trying not to be anyone's mortal enemy . . . I know that each one of us carries the plague within us . . . and that we must continually watch ourselves to avoid breathing into another's face in a fit of absent-mindedness, and giving him the infection."

It is good to know how wicked, stubborn, lucid we can be and how much we can love evil. Doubtless most of our faults are primarily faults due to weakness. If they were acknowledged and mended, they would not constitute an obstacle to God. Far from it; as in the case of many saints, they would serve as a springboard for our trust in him, for our humility. The obstacle to God within us is our pride. Pride consists in wanting to do without God. It is our pride which makes out of sins of weakness sins of malice. Out of spite we boast of the error which we had inadvertently committed. So as not to reverse engines, we continue to do purposely what we had begun through absent-mindedness or negligence, to pursue wickedly what we had begun stupidly, just to avoid admitting that we had gone astray.

Thus it sometimes happens that we get into the wrong bus. We boarded it, lightly, resolutely, easily, confidently. Suddenly, certain imperceptible signs — we don't exactly know which — make us feel that we have made a mistake, that we should have boarded another, that we are not going in the right direction. Then we say to ourselves: "I could ask where this bus is going and eventually get down before it goes too far, otherwise I will never get in time to those friends who have invited me to dinner." But at once we picture ourselves blushing as we walk through the whole compartment and we see the mocking glances of our fellow-travellers. "Oh, he took the wrong bus!" So rather than face such humiliation, we keep to our corner, paralysed with worry. However, the journey continues and we travel through districts which are stranger and stranger to us. Then we begin to say: "It can't be helped. I won't be able to reach those friends in time for a meal. I will get there later and will have to invent some excuse to explain it. I will pretend I understood they were only expecting me for coffee." And the bus still goes on. Now, in the twilight, the countryside looks dismal, we pass quarries where they are carving tombstones, strange factories, waste land. The inhabitants look more and more threatening. The travellers who board the bus have a sinister look; it seems that they know that you have made a mistake and that they are sneering about it amongst themselves. We feel that we have gone so far, so terribly far, that we can't even hope to spend any part of the evening with our friends who are waiting for us over there, under the cheerful light of the table lamps and with the meal ready. "Then I will have to think of something else to explain my absence . . . What a nuisance! But after all, why should I go to so much trouble? They had no need to invite me this evening. And after all, I don't know these people. And they don't really care to see me. Why did they invite me? It's all a game. They will feel obliged to phone me tomorrow. Never mind, I won't answer the phone . . . And I will no longer open letters . . . and I will never go to dinner with anyone . . . and I would like this bus to run off the road and for everything to end. Life is too complicated . . ."

If he had had the courage to get down as soon as he realized his mistake, if he had hurried along to take the right bus, our man would have got there a little late, but his friends—who would have begun to get worried—would have been delighted and relieved to see him arrive all the same! And he would have been so pleased to tell them all about it and say: "Fancy, I almost didn't get here, I made a mistake." And they would have replied: "It was lucky that you noticed it in time. It was lucky you had the courage to jump from that bus, and that you preferred to come to us at all costs."

Damnation is to prefer to be unhappy all on our own.

117

To damn ourselves is to fall into the evil which we see, the evil which we suffer but of which we refuse to repent for fear of suffering even more. We prefer the certainty of being unhappy all on our own to the possibility of being happy with another, with others. Because "possibly" it hurts.

When we are happy with others, all that part of ourselves which we disclose to them becomes vulnerable, and we have to give up being self-sufficient, independent. We must give up for ever that hollow peace for which we yearn because we believe we could achieve it without the help of anyone. "You will be God, you will need no one, you will be satisfied with yourself alone", whispered the devil to Adam.

We receive heaven. We make hell ourselves by making ourselves unhappy. We are well aware that we could start to believe, to hope, to love. But we would have once more to be dependent, to wait, communicate, confess to begin with that we had made a mistake. So we prefer to remain on our pillow of despair on which evil in the end may perhaps be lulled. And if it is not lulled, then we will try to forget, we will bestir ourselves, we will work, we will try to deafen ourselves, so as not to hear within us that hell of sterility, wickedness, harshness, bitterness which whips us towards "amusements", towards our wretched pleasures, towards oblivion and towards death.

There are two ways in which we can react to our own falls. Either we say: "It is not worth while getting up because I will only fall again. It is too difficult for me. I don't know how to love. I find it too hard to believe all my life. I will never manage to persevere until the end. So I might just as well stay there now. I am fed up with suffering and with continually reopening the wound which

I do not know how to heal." Or on the contrary: "It's not worth while remaining on the ground. It will end all the same by my getting up. Because God is so good that however long, however wickedly I remain without moving, however great my bad faith and my ill will, however harsh, however hostile I may show myself to him, he will not allow me to remain there. He will not accept the idea of leaving me without casting a look back. He will harass me, he will call me until I can no longer remain silent and allow myself to die, until I can no longer be all alone. Then, as I will repent all the same, I might as well start at once. I might as well confess at once. I might as well allow myself to be consoled at once. I may as well allow myself to rejoice at once!"

There is only one way of curing sadness — of being delivered from evil — that is not to love it.

Eucharist

IF THE saying of the Our Father is already a kind of liturgical office, if it is true that we fulfil a function which has been entrusted to us every time we ask with faith that the name be hallowed, the kingdom come, the will be done, that the bread be given each day, forgiveness be received and given, that evil be set aside . . . there is a chosen place to celebrate the Our Father — the Mass.

What is the Mass? The Mass is Eucharist, thanksgiving, gratitude, the solemn restitution to God of the gifts he has made to us, the joyful passage (Pasch) of the world towards God. "Before the festival day of the pasch, Jesus knowing that his hour was come, that he should pass out of this world to the Father . . ."[1]

Eucharist means restitution. "Who the day before he suffered . . . giving thanks to thee . . ." At the Consecration, Jesus gives himself. Later on, "By him, and with him and in him", it is our turn. Jesus — in the Mass — gives back our lives to the Father with his own, just as in the Communion he gives us the life of the Father with his

[1] John 13:1.

own. "You shall know that I am in my Father and you in me and I in you."[2]

The more we receive, the more we have to give back. And the more we give back, the more we shall be given and the more we shall have to continue to give back. It is an endless chain or rather an uninterrupted game, in which the only fault is to keep the ball.

At the Elevation, Christ is shown. But to see something that is shown to us does not commit us. On the other hand, the amen at the end of the Canon (the "minor elevation") does place us right inside, it makes us part of the gift, it makes us join the passage, the pasch, it consecrates us. It is an act of thanksgiving . . . with him, in him, "Amen".

It is exactly at that moment that the Our Father had to come. "Urged by our Saviour's bidding and schooled . . ." (We have just learnt it once more, we have again been urged, we are schooled further each time), we make bold to say: "Our Father".

From the moment we say "Father" we give up all our rebellious will. "Hallowed be thy name." Prefer thy name, I know it means giving up ours; prefer thy kingdom, I know it means giving up bothering about ours; to want thy will means accepting to care no longer about ours. There are as many sacrifices as there are requests: sacrifices of praise.

"It is a terrible thing to fall into the hands of the living God", said St. Paul. Because a living God is a God who loves, a God whose love has led him to where all living love leads: to the nailing on the Cross. A God who dreams of nothing else but sharing his own destiny, his

[2] John 14:20.

121

crucifying beatitude, with those he loves. What better fate could God think of giving us than his own? This is the gift, the grace, the joy which we have accepted at the Mass, at the Eucharist, at the thanksgiving.

The Our Father is a Eucharist, a placing of ourselves absolutely at God's disposal, an absolute restitution, an absolute opening of our arms, an absolute assent, an absolute agreement. At that precise moment, we are no longer of this world ("My kingdom is not of this world"). We have *passed* for the space of a prayer, into his own.

God is gift, God is effusion of himself. Creation, the incarnation, the redemption are efforts which he has made to come near us. At Mass we can "give back" to him love for love, joy for joy.

We too can be restitution, Eucharist. It is the answer, the second half, the success of God's gesture. "All that is thine is mine." God has given himself. "And all that is mine is thine", we reply. God will not have thrown his love to us in vain. God will not have risked his call in vain, our loyalties answer him: "All that is mine is thine, thy will be done, thy kingdom come . . . hallowed be . . ." And this answer enables him to begin anew that which makes his joy, to begin anew to give us what we have given back to him, his life, his love, his beatitude, his Son.

This movement of Eucharist, of passage, is in itself the most joyful act in the world. It makes us consistent with our real nature, it makes us again that filial and assenting being which we become every time we agree to be a new creature, every time we agree, having given everything back, to receive everything again. It gives us back to God and to ourselves, to the creature God wanted us to be. The Eucharist is the most profoundly natural

movement of man, because it is the most natural movement of God, his very breathing.

It is the Father who gives life; it is the Son who gives
back his life. God is he who gives life. We could never
achieve it in spite of all our efforts. He had given the
breath of life to Adam who had kept it, refused it, lost
it. The Son, the new Adam, has given it back. The Son
has given up the breath. "Into thy hands I commend my
spirit."[3] Then the Father gave a new Breath at Pentecost.
This is the Spirit that quickens us.

All the life of humanity is the story of this Breath:
breath on Adam to create him, of Jesus to give himself up;
breath of God to re-create us; breath which is increasingly
imparted to whoever allows himself to be stimulated, to
whoever allows himself to be swept into the rhythm of
this divine breathing. To pray is to learn how to breathe,
to perceive the breath, and having received it, to give it
back with the same transport of joy which had raised us for
this aspiration of our whole being. To aspire, then to
expire as Jesus expired on the cross. To surrender, to
give ourselves up.

"We should listen to the breathing of the worlds", said
Hello. And to hear it we must go so far "that we can no
longer remember any of the sounds they make", even the
sound of our own footsteps. So far away. There, where we
shall do what Adam did not do, that filial gesture which
places at God's disposal everything that he has given us;
there, where we will say: "Father, thy will be done"; there,
where every morning we perform Eucharist, everywhere
where we entrust ourselves to the Father "at all times, in all
places", where overcoming terror, anguish and tears, like

[3] Luke 23:46.

a child calming down after a fit of sobbing, we begin again to breathe in his arms; we abandon ourselves, we surrender ourselves at last to him.

In the dialogue at the foot of the altar, there is an echo of our anxiety: "Soul, why art thou downcast, why art thou all lament?" and the server replies: *"Spera in Deo"*. Come on, hope once more in God. Open your hands, drop everything, throw yourself into the void. Give back your life to enable God to give you his. Our Eucharists, alas, are often as phony as our contritions and our communions. This is the reason why most of our Masses are so lifeless. We pretend to celebrate the pasch before people who pretend to consent to it. Sometimes, before beginning, one feels like asking the congregation: "Are you really keen? Wouldn't you prefer to postpone it? Wait a little . . . until you believe in it? Until you no longer see it as a formality where we take advantage of Another's sacrifice to avoid having to make one ourselves?"

It is said that the "Amen" that replied to the *Per ipsum et cum ipso et in ipso* used to roll like a clap of thunder in the churches of Rome. Now, a dismal silence follows the sound of the bell which wakes us up for the Our Father.

Who are those who come to Mass to try and die? To train for that last Eucharist which will be our death? Who is it who would wish his kingdom to come during the Mass? Who dreams that it may be the end of the world? Mass is a passage (pasch). When going there we should say: "The hour is come. We are going to pass from this world to the Father." This is how the first Mass started. "Jesus knowing that his hour was come, that he should pass out of this world to the Father . . . and that

124

he came from God and goeth to God."[4] Are our Masses great homecomings? Every time we celebrate the Mass properly "until he comes" we hasten the advent of the Lord. "When the Eucharist is celebrated all over the earth, then this world will pass and the Lord will manifest himself in all his glory."

After the early Christians had received communion, they used to kneel down and say: "Lord, may this world pass now and may your kingdom come." They had sincerely made the passage; they had celebrated the Eucharist. They would have preferred not to retrace their steps. Henceforth they felt more at home in that other kingdom to which they had "sacrificed" all that was dearest to them. The Mass should "naturalize" us to the things of the Father.

"Father . . . that the world may know that thou hast loved them as thou hast also loved me. Father I will that where I am, they also whom thou hast given me may be with me."[5] To be loved like Jesus, share his fate, be where he is . . . Who are those who would stay for that Mass? Who have sufficient filial devotion to go and expose themselves in this way, unreservedly, to the devouring love of the Father? To go with the Son and taste that fullness of joy and learn what it means to obey?

"Holy Father . . . now I come to thee: and these things I speak in the world that they may have my joy filled in themselves."[6] "As thou, Father, in me and I in thee: that they also may be one in us."[7] The celebrant at Mass is a ferryman. If we really believed this, would we be so enthusiastic? Instead, would we not all hold him back by the hem of his chasuble, clinging closely together to ensure

---

[4] John 13:1, 3.   [5] John 17:23-24.   [6] John 17:11-13.
[7] John 17:21.

that it doesn't happen? This time we would be "one", to avoid losing ourselves at once in them, to be quite sure to remain on this side! Our presence at Mass, instead of being an assistance, is more often a real sabotage (sabotage means: making a noise with sabots. And is it not true that many spend their Mass, patiently stamping their feet as they wait for it to end?).

The Mass is the central act of Creation — paradise re-gained — the opportunity given each day to every one of us to become the praise which God expects. "And I am glorified in them", a mystery of Faith *(mysterium fidei),* for a few faithful who come to accept again their condition as sons. The essential act of the Mass is to get back into this dependency, to come and say to the Father that we are happy to depend on him, that even if we could, we would not want to escape from it, that we know that we will find our truest, deepest love in praise, in obedience, in the Eucharist.

Family parties have the same meaning: when the children entertain their parents, it is, without knowing it, to express their joy, their wish to choose them after having received them, their wish to transform a fortuitous, obligatory dependence, into a dependence that they want, love and desire. Thus, the Mass transforms a dependence which we suffer into a dependence which we take on, which we prefer to any other condition, it transposes our — profane — powerlessness into a sacred subordination. Each morning at Mass, we come to choose to die. We choose what will come: suffering, failures, disappointments or successes, it matters not. We come to "sacrifice" (make sacred) everything, consecrate everything. Everything must be reconsecrated every day because everything, every day — even our good works — is profaned.

126

We must not escape free from Mass. We must leave something there. The meaning of the Offertory is to strip ourselves of a piece of that armour which protects us against God. When the ancients offered a bullock or a bull, they offered an instrument of work. It meant: "Lord, I believe that thou art more useful to me even to pull my plough, than this bullock which I sacrifice to thee. I know that thou art stronger to protect me against adversity than my money, my wealth, my weapons, than everything that I can imagine to defend myself. I prefer to entrust the care of my life to thee."

We have invented symbolic offerings. But what is symbolic is always taken back. What about giving something for keeps! Just imagine what a face the children would make if their father were to say: "Listen, we are going to make a real offering. We have no bulls, no horses, but we have a car which we can do without. We are therefore going to offer it to the parish priest for the use of the Church. Later on, at the Offertory, I will go and place the ignition key on the altar; and for the first time the Mass will really be for us the celebration of a sacrifice in which we have taken part. And you must believe, we must believe, that this Mass will enrich us infinitely more than all the excursions, all the trips which we could still have made in this car, since we have given it over to God." We see the picture: the children aghast, furious: "But he's going mad." "And we will have to be present at that Mass? We will have to see it all, see that priest accept the key of our car? And after that, watch others drive in it all the summer, reclining on the cushions while we go on foot?" It makes them sick, life seems no longer worth living. That very moment they are ready for the kingdom to come! What does it matter to them if everything goes bust. Life without

127

a car (and God knows what father will think of next, now that he has started on that track!) seems more distasteful to them than the end of the world.

Whatever be the gift we are asked to make, we have to believe that at every one of our Masses, we will receive infinitely more than we have offered. But we never reach God except as the result of a sacrifice, as the result of something which we have thrown to him, the weight of which drags us behind it, like a dear one whom we have given up and who awaits us. We must throw our treasure so that our heart may plunge into God: "For where thy treasure is, there is thy heart also."[8]

All those who have discarded their trust in themselves, in their strength, in their talents, in their possessions, to place it in God and in him alone, have gladdened the heart of the Father in the way the Son wished them to do. "Call him Father." Ask him for your daily bread instead of worrying so much, do his will instead of asking him for hours to do yours. Ask him to forgive instead of trying, day after day, to save face. Entrust him with the care of delivering you from evil, like children, like sons.

In the Eucharist, the Son associates us with the cult which he renders to his Father. On Calvary, we have seen how God loves, we have had the revelation of the eternal beatitude of God. The Eucharist enables us to participate in it. Through the Eucharist we can become participants, associated already here below with the fine courtesies of the house of God. "Father, all that is thine is mine, all that is mine is thine." — "Thy will be done."

Every time we are crucified and willing, torn but acquiescent — happy, unhappy — we begin to savour the

[8] Matt. 6:21.

128

heavenly beatitude. Then we can say: "Father, in spite of all this evil which frightens me, because I trust thee, see . . . in my heart thy name is hallowed, thy kingdom is desired, thy will is cherished, awaited, respected. In this state of bitterness, my bread — that which sustains me, comforts me — is to know that through thy Son something perfect is ceaselessly accomplished beyond all our imperfections, that thy will *is* done through him in the eternal Eucharist, and also amongst us already every time that we make room for him, every time the Eucharist is celebrated somewhere on earth, as in heaven."

The only absolute promise that God has made us is that the Our Father will be said, the Eucharist will be made, until the end of time. He has not guaranteed us against weakness or sin. But whatever our aberrations may be, we will always begin again to say the Our Father, to make Eucharist, to celebrate a holy sacrifice, which the eternal sacrifice of Christ will always make valid.

Whilst it is discouraging to think of all our ignorance, all our questionable actions, the corruption of all our works, the imposture of our successes, the hypocrisy of most of our gestures, it is consoling to know that there is Someone amongst us who always says the Mass perfectly, and that, through him it is possible for us to cling to something that is just, something that is pure.

We need only follow, "serve", his dialogue with the Father, look at him, give thanks and consent. We are only asked to answer — with him, in him — "Amen!" There is nothing for us to invent.

The true imitation of Jesus Christ is the Mass — where, "Urged by our Saviour's bidding and schooled by his divine ordinance, we make bold to say: Our Father . . ."